THE INVESTOR'S
GUIDE TO
ECONOMIC INDICATORS

THE INVESTOR'S
GUIDE TO
ECONOMIC INDICATORS

Charles R. Nelson

John Wiley & Sons

New York   Chichester   Brisbane   Toronto   Singapore

This publication is designed to provide accurate and
authoritative information in regard to the subject
matter covered. It is sold with the understanding that
the publisher is not engaged in rendering legal, accounting,
or other professional service. If legal advice or other
expert assistance is required, the services of a competent
professional person should be sought. *From a Declaration
of Principles jointly adopted by a Committee of the
American Bar Association and a Committee of Publishers.*

Library of Congress Cataloging-in-Publication Data:
Nelson, Charles R.
  The investor's guide to economic indicators.

  Bibliography: p.
  1. Economic indicators—United States.
2. Investments—United States. I. Title.

HC106.8.N38 1987   330.973'0927   87−2134
ISBN 0−471−85902−8
ISBN 0−471−51329−6 pbk.

Printed in the United States of America
10 9 8 7 6 5 4 3 2

Acknowledgments

Many people have contributed to the development of this book and most are unaware of how helpful they have been. The good people at Stein Roe and Farnham showed me the importance of relating economics to investment decisions, and I have learned a great deal through my interaction with them over the past 15 years. I am grateful to the American Association of Independent Investors for letting me use their educational seminars as a forum for trying this material out on its intended audience. Trinity College of Cambridge University provided a beautiful setting and the facilities that allowed me to draft this book while I was a Visiting Fellow Commoner. And thanks to President Reagan and Federal Reserve Board Chairman Paul Volcker for keeping the dollar strong during my year in England! My wife, Kate, has encouraged me throughout because she feels, as I do, that economists make far too little effort to make their work understandable to the public. Antoinette Wills has been an excellent editorial

Acknowledgments

adviser and the source of many good ideas. Amber Curtis and Laura Cordy provided expert word processing. My colleague Potluri Rao developed the graphics software that I used. Sharon Tighe did an excellent job of preparing the Index. Finally, I would never have written this book, or much of anything, without the infinite patience of my mother, Julia Hydar Nelson, who taught me through comment and example how to write. She is still my best critic, as she showed by her extensive constructive comments on the manuscript of this book.

C.R.N

Contents

Acknowledgments, v

Introduction, 1

1. Interest Rates: The Long and the Short of It, 7

2. Inflation, or How Fast Do I Have to Run Just to
   Stand Still?, 21

3. Money and the Fed: Can You Have Too Much of
   a Good Thing?, 29

4. Have Interest Rates Been High, Really?, 39

5. The Stock Market: Refuge from Inflation, or
   Trap?, 49

6. The Real Economy, 57

7. Profits, Real Profits, and Really Real Profits, 69

8. What Is the Future of American Business
   Worth? 83

9. Indicators That Forecast the Real Economy, 95

10. Indicators for Stock Market Timing, 119

11. That Scary Federal Deficit: Will We Ever Get Rid
    of It?, 143

Contents

12. **The Other Deficit: Our Foreign Trade Gap, 169**

The Calendar of Important Indicators, 184

Index, 185

THE INVESTOR'S
GUIDE TO
ECONOMIC INDICATORS

Introduction

One of the toughest challenges facing the individual investor is how to keep on top of developments in the economy and how to relate them to investment decisions. Fortunately, the U.S. government is a prodigious producer of indicators of the state of the economy, the alphabet soup of GNP, M1, M2, CPI, PPI, and so forth. Little is done, however, by the government or by the media to put these indicators in a meaningful perspective for the investor.

How can you interpret these indicators to understand better what is going on in the economy? Which indicators are worth paying attention to and which are not? How do they relate to each other to make up a meaningful picture of the economy? How do they relate to investment results in the financial markets? These are the basic questions this book addresses.

You do not need a graduate degree in economics to discern the important trends in the economy and understand their significance for investment. It is sometimes said that "economics is common sense made complicated" and academic economics is often just that. In this book I have tried to replace the jargon of professional economists with a commonsense approach, using simple charts to show how the important indicators of the economy can be interpreted.

There is no question that we live in an age of information overload—there is more of it than we know what to do with. It is more essential than ever to know which economic and investment indicators are the most important and why. This book emphasizes understanding the economic environment using indicators that are announced in the media. It is not an encyclopedia or compendium of every statistic known to economists. No human can make intelligent use of the reams of numbers that government and private agencies produce. To try to understand the economy by looking at all the indicators would be like trying to understand astronomy by looking up at the Arizona night sky. The array is dazzling but completely overwhelming. What we need is a simple star chart that points out the key features. This book aims to be a guide for the individual investor to the key features of our economy.

Investors, as compared to savers, make their own investment decisions based on their own analysis of their financial position and of the investment climate. They make use of expert opinion but they realize that experts generally have their own ax to grind. Stockbrokers, after all, make their living from commissions on purchases and sales of stocks, not on investment results. People selling limited partnerships, insurance, or annuities likewise have an interest in convincing you to buy their product. The economists working for brokerage firms, banks, and insurance companies are worth listening to for their appraisals of the economy and financial markets, but they too understand the sources of their employers' profits. These firms are, of course, all trying to attract the investor's dollars. Economists in government are advisors to the administration, but they are also propagandists for its economic policies and defenders of its record. The investor needs to look at all expert economic and financial opinion with a skeptical eye and ultimately form his or her own view of what is happening in the economy and the impact it will have on investments. Survival as an investor requires no less.

My objective here is to make the stream of economic news and information that we receive daily from television and the financial press more valuable to you as an investor. It is easy to feel overwhelmed by the volume of information that the media throw at us and at a loss to know how it fits together into a meaningful picture of the economic environment. It is also easy to feel intimidated by the facile jargon of the experts who give the impression that they know a lot more than you do. I hope that after reading this book you will feel that you have a better understanding of the economy we live in today, where it is headed, and why. The result should be better investment and business decisions and the peace of mind that comes with having more control over your own financial destiny.

Economic indicators are among the most valuable tools that an investor has, if he or she knows how to use them. For an economic indicator to be useful to the investor it must satisfy three basic criteria. The first and most important is *relevance*. Which are the most important economic indicators for making investment decisions? What do they tell us about trends in the economy and how does that relate to the financial markets? A second important criterion is *timely release*. An indicator has to be announced soon enough to be of use. Some of the most widely publicized indicators are among the least satisfactory in this respect. Fortunately, other more timely indicators are available if you know what they are. A third key criterion is *availability*. The most useful indicators are those published in the financial press as soon as they are released. Other indicators of potential use to investors appear in government publications that take a couple of months to reach subscribers. The fourth criterion is *stability*. An indicator that wiggles all over the place is of limited value. There is little point, for example, in losing sleep over the significance of the money supply numbers announced by the Federal Reserve Board every Thursday. Whether M1 is up or down depends too much on special circumstances that week and tells us little, if anything, about the direction of Federal Reserve policy. It makes much more sense to monitor indicators on a monthly basis, particularly looking to see what the trend has been over the past year. I have emphasized a long term perspective by designing the charts in this book to show how indicators have related to the economy over the past 25 years. In the often confusing world of rapidly changing economic conditions, that long term perspective is one of the most important advantages an investor can have.

We begin with interest rates in Chapter 1 because they are basic to understanding the investment climate and how it has changed in the past 25 years. We will see that the spread between long term and short term interest rates often points out the future direction of interest rates. Inflation has hurt many investors and benefited others. Chapter 2 looks at indicators of inflation and at warning signals of future inflation—or deflation. In Chapter 3 we look at where inflation comes from and see why money supply growth has tended to foreshadow major moves in inflation by about two years. In Chapter 4 we look at interest rates again, but this time in *real* terms—net of inflation. Will ''easy money'' policies by the Federal Reserve Board lead to lower interest rates or higher ones?

In Chapter 5 we take a sobering look at how the purchasing power of stock market investments fared during the stormy 1970s and 1980s. The fortunes of investors depend not only on the *monetary economy* of interest rates and inflation but also on the *real economy* of manufacturing and trade. The performance of the real economy comes under scrutiny in Chapter 6. The real economy produces the corporate profits that make dividends possible and that give stocks value. These linkages are explored in Chapters 7 and 8. Leading indicators can help you see the future direction of the economy and inflation. I give my views on which to watch and why in Chapter 9. Indicators for stock market timing are the subject of Chapter 10 and we look at the record of some that have worked pretty well. The last two Chapters, 11 and 12, examine those twin deficits that seem destined to plague our economy in the 1980s: the budget deficit of the federal government and our foreign trade deficit. How did we get into this deficit mess and what are its implications for investors? What would it take to get out of it and what are the chances that we will?

I hope that you find the game of economy-watching as fascinating and rewarding as I do.

1

Interest Rates:
The Long and the Short of It

Why start with interest rates? Because they are fundamental to investment itself. *Interest rate* and *yield* are two terms for the same thing: the percentage increase on money invested in a security that promises fixed cash payments in the future. These securities are called *fixed income securities* to distinguish them from common stocks that pay a dividend that varies with the fortunes of the company. Fixed income securities generally *mature* on a specific date in the future, at which time a final payment is made to the investor. If this maturity date is within one year of the date the security is purchased, it is called a *short term* or *money market* security, and the interest rate earned on it is a short term interest rate or short term yield. If the maturity date is years in the future, then the security is called a bond. The yield on a bond is fixed for the life of the bond and is called a *long term interest rate* or *long term yield*.

The short term securities you are most likely to encounter as a private investor are those issued by the U.S. Treasury, called *Treasury bills*, and those issued by banks, and savings and loans, called *certificates of deposit* (CDs). Those issued by industrial companies are called *commercial paper* and are typically held by institutional investors, such as money market mutual funds, who are better able to appraise the creditworthiness of the issuer. As an individual investor you can purchase Treasury bills from your bank or directly from any Federal Reserve Bank branch. The U.S. Treasury holds an auction of bills every week, and a large fraction of these bills mature in 90 days, although maturities of up to 360 days are sometimes offered.

Because of the great quantity of 90-day Treasury bills offered for sale, the creditworthiness of the issuer (the government is the only debtor with the power to tax its creditors!), and the very competitive nature of the market for these bills, the yield on the 90-day Treasury bill has become the bellwether indicator of short term interest rates. How are these yields calculated? The first thing to realize is that the bill is a very simple security that promises to do only one thing: pay its face value on the maturity date. No interest payments are made in the meantime. The smallest face value amount issued is $10,000. These bills are simply a promise to pay the sum of $10,000 on the 90th day following delivery of the bill. In order for the purchaser to gain by holding a bill, its cost must be less than its face value. This cost to the purchaser is determined in the marketplace by competition among investors. Suppose that you can buy a 90-day bill today for $9750. In 90 days the Treasury will pay you $10,000, which is $250 more than your cost. Your percentage gain is $250 ÷ $9750 × 100%, or about 2½%. Sound low? Remember that it only takes one quarter of a year to earn the 2½%. If you reinvested your money three more times at the same interest rate, you would have earned a total of about 10 percent over a year's time. This is called the *annualized yield* and is always used as the basis for quoting yields in order to put other yields for securities of different maturities on a comparable footing. Yields on U.S. Treasury bills are quoted daily in the financial press.

Bonds issued by the U.S. Treasury are likewise the bellwethers for long term interest rates. Any bond is a promise to make regular "coupon" payments, generally twice a year, plus a final payment of the amount of the face value of the bond on a stated maturity date some years in the future. The coupon rate (stated as a percent of face value per annum), the face value amount, and the maturity date tell you all there is to know about what you will receive if you buy the bond. For example, if you buy the U.S. Treasury's 12 percent bond of the year 2010 with a face value of $10,000, you will receive $600 every six months until 2010 when the Treasury will make a final payment of $10,000. Bonds issued by companies and local governments have the same basic characteristics as a Treasury bond, except that the ability of these issuers to make the promised payments is less certain. The yield on a bond is the percentage return to the bond-holder over the life of the bond. This *yield to maturity* is made up of two parts: (1) the yield due to the fixed coupon, and (2) the difference between the cost of the bond and the final face value payment averaged, or *amortized*, over the life of the bond. It is important to realize that the cost of the bond to you as an investor is not fixed by the Treasury, but rather, it is determined in the marketplace. It may be above or below the face value.

Let's take the example of the 12 percent Treasury bond of 2010 to see how bond prices and yields are related. This bond pays its owner $1200 per year with a face value of $10,000. Suppose that this bond is currently priced in the market at $10,000. Since there is no difference between the cost of the bond to the investor and the ultimate face value payment, the yield to maturity consists entirely of coupon yield: $1200 ÷ $10,000 × 100% or 12% per annum. This tells us that the long term interest rate is 12 percent. Suppose now that the long term interest rate rises to 13 percent; what will happen to the price of this bond in the marketplace? The price must fall, of course, because the bond still pays only $1200 per year. If the price fell to $9230 the coupon yield would be 13 percent since $1200 ÷ $9230 × 100% = 13%. The price need not fall quite that much because the purchaser of the bond also benefits from the appreciation in the value of the bond as it goes from today's price to its final value of $10,000 at maturity. *What is clear is that rising long term interest rates imply falling bond prices—and vice versa.* The exact calculations need not concern us because the yield to maturity on each U.S. Treasury bond is computed daily and published in the financial press under the heading *yield*. This yield on representative Treasury bonds tells us that the basic long term interest rate is in the economy. This establishes the minimum cost of long term funds to private borrowers and the assured safe long term return to investors.

The fundamental difference between short term and long term securities is this: A short term security provides stability of value over the short term but does not provide assurance of yield over the long term. In contrast, a long term security may fluctuate in market value over the short term, but it guarantees a fixed yield over the long term. If you buy a 90-day bill, you know that you will have exactly $10,000 ninety days later. You will then be obliged to accept whatever yield is available in the marketplace if you wish to reinvest your capital. If short term rates fall from 10 percent to 5 percent you will probably wish you had purchased a long term security. If you buy a long term bond you know exactly what yield you will earn over the life of the bond. However, if long term interest rates rise over the next few months, the market value of your bond will fall. If that happens, you will probably wish you had bought a bill instead so that you could reinvest the proceeds at the higher yields being offered. If interest rates fall, you will see a rise in the market value of your bond, and you will be able to congratulate yourself on having had the foresight to lock in those higher yields!

Let's take a look now at what has happened to the short and long term interest rates available to investors—and faced by borrowers—over the past quarter century. Our indicator of short term rates is the yield on 90-day U.S. Treasury bills. Figure 1 is a chart of these yields, which are recorded each month. Individual points are connected to form a solid line. The height of the line gives the interest rate in percentage points indicated on the scale at the left of the chart. Now, we all know that interest rates have risen a lot in the 1970s, but it is still sobering to see the sweeping upward march of short term rates from below 3 percent in the early 1960s to 8 percent in the mid-1970s, and then to a peak of about 16 percent in 1981. They plummeted sharply in the 1982 economic slump and since then have retraced much of their 1970s ascent. This roller coaster ride in basic short term investment yields is indicative of the wrenching changes that have shaken the investment world in the last 25 years.

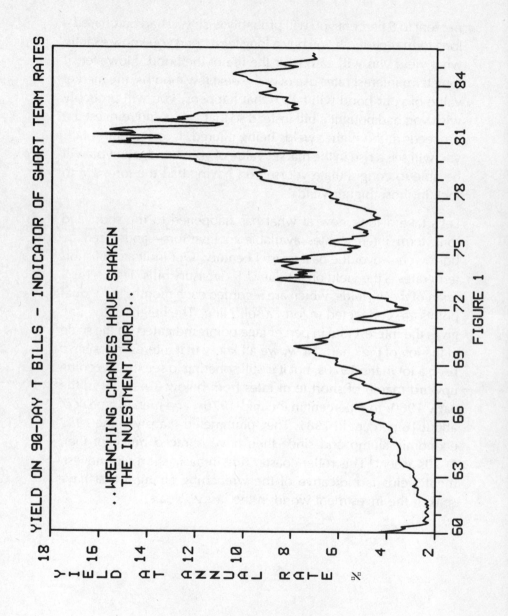

YIELD ON 90-DAY T BILLS - INDICATOR OF SHORT TERM RATES

..WRENCHING CHANGES HAVE SHAKEN
THE INVESTMENT WORLD..

FIGURE 1

Interest Rates: The Long and the Short of It

Our indicator of long term interest rates is the yield on U.S. Treasury bonds, and Figure 2 shows what has happened in the long term market over the past quarter century. Clearly the trend was relentlessly upward until 1981, with long rates rising from a steady 4 percent in the early 1960s to the 7 percent area in the 1970s to a peak of about 14 percent in late 1981. What was happening to investors in long term bonds as yields more than tripled? They were getting killed! Existing bonds, those in investors' portfolios, were being marked down in the marketplace to keep up with the ever higher yields being offered on newly issued bonds. Those investors who sold their bonds almost surely suffered a capital loss. Those who held on received a lower return than they would have had they invested instead in short term securities, which would have allowed them to reinvest their capital every 90 days or so at ever higher rates. It is not coincidental that money market mutual funds, which are bundles of Treasury bills and commercial paper, developed and prospered during this period! Individual investors and institutions wanted the safety that short term securities offered.

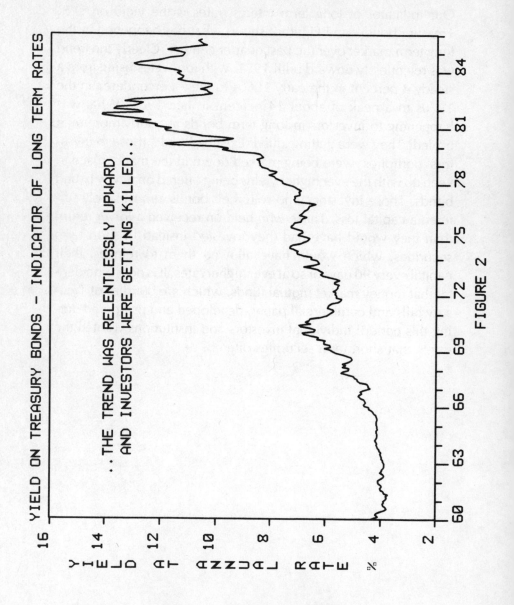

YIELD ON TREASURY BONDS - INDICATOR OF LONG TERM RATES

..THE TREND WAS RELENTLESSLY UPWARD
AND INVESTORS WERE GETTING KILLED..

FIGURE 2

Interest Rates: The Long and the Short of It

When the two interest rate indicators are superimposed, as in Figure 3, it is apparent that long and short rates are rarely the same. Sometimes short rates are above long rates, sometimes below. Why are they not just the same? Notice also that long rates bounce around much less than short rates do—they are less volatile. Why should this be so? The answer to both these questions lies in the nature of the choice confronting long term investors. If I buy a bond, I am entitled to a fixed rate of return over the life of the bond. An alternative strategy is to buy short term securities such as Treasury bills and reinvest the proceeds in new short term securities as the old ones mature. To make the choice, I need to decide what I think short term yields are going to be in the future when it is time to roll over my portfolio into new securities. This is, of course, purely a matter of expectations about future short term interest rates.

For example, in late 1976 short term rates were well below their peak levels of 1974, having dropped from nearly nine percent to about 4½ percent. Long term rates had eased a bit over this period but were still around 6½ percent, leaving a gap of about two percent between long and short rates. Why were investors willing to buy a bill yielding 4½ percent when they could buy a bond yielding 6½ percent? The answer is *expectations*. Investors perceived that short term rates were only temporarily low and would be rising again as the economy continued its recovery from the 1974 recession. While the bond-holder was assured of 6½ percent over the life of the bond, the bill-holder expected to benefit from a rising trend in short term rates over the next several years, and indeed did so! In fact, the bill-holder came out way ahead during the subsequent five years of rising interest rates, while the bond-holder took substantial losses. Keep in mind that the bill-holder was able to reinvest at the end of each

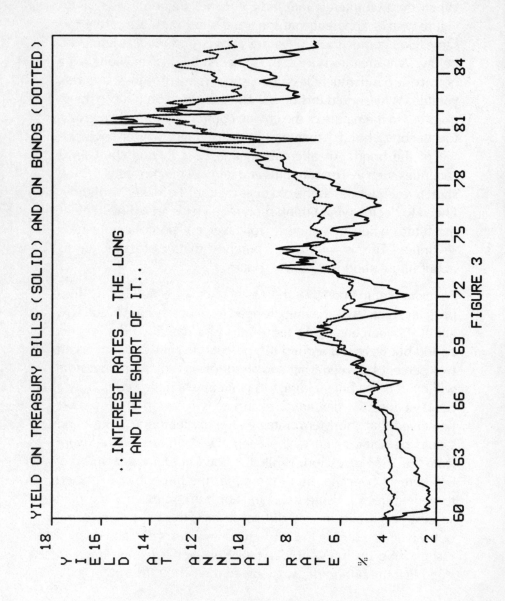

YIELD ON TREASURY BILLS (SOLID) AND ON BONDS (DOTTED)

..INTEREST RATES - THE LONG
AND THE SHORT OF IT..

FIGURE 3

three-month period at the ever-rising yields that the market offered during the next five years. This process of investors balancing long term rates against the anticipated future level of short rates, rather than against the current level, is what tends to iron out the peaks and valleys, so that long rates move more smoothly and more slowly than do short rates. Investors are willing to accept a long term rate that is lower than the short rate when short rates are perceived to be temporarily high, but they require a long term rate that is higher than the short rate when short rates are perceived to be temporarily low.

If the long term interest rate reflects investors' collective forecast of where short term interest rates are headed in the future, then the spread between long and short rates should predict the future direction of interest rates. It does! The spread is charted in Figure 4. Times like early 1977, when long rates were well above short rates were also times when short rates were poised for a subsequent rise. Notice particularly 1960, 1967, 1971, 1972, 1977, 1980, and 1982. Similarly, times when long rates were well below short rates, producing a negative spread, were times when short rates were poised for a sharp fall. This was evident during 1966, 1969, 1974, early 1980, and 1981. Each of these troughs in the spread was followed by a drop in short term interest rates.

What about the large positive spread during much of 1984 and 1985? Evidently, the market (investors collectively) expected short term rates to rise during 1985. The market was wrong this time! Short term rates dropped about 3½ percent points from August 1984 to the end of 1985. When short term rates turn out to be lower than investors anticipated, their expectations for future short term rates tend to be revised downward. Since long term bonds then look more attractive, their prices are bid up and their yields fall. This adjustment restores the balance between long

---

17

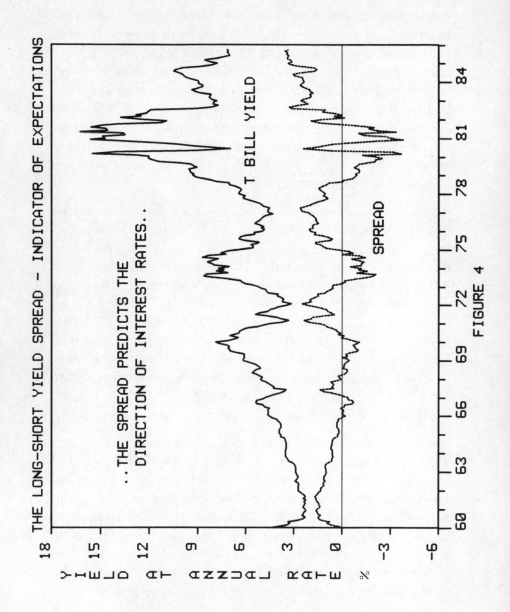

THE LONG-SHORT YIELD SPREAD – INDICATOR OF EXPECTATIONS

..THE SPREAD PREDICTS THE
DIRECTION OF INTEREST RATES..

T BILL YIELD

SPREAD

FIGURE 4

YIELD AT ANNUAL RATE %

18 15 12 9 6 3 0 -3 -6

60 63 66 69 72 75 78 81 84

and short term rates. It is at such times that bond-holders reap a capital gain because the market value of their bond portfolio rises. Indeed, investors who felt that short term rates were not likely to rise in 1985, and therefore held bonds, profited from one of the greatest bond market rallies of this century. How could you have seen that the market was likely to be wrong? We'll get to that in Chapter 6.

The Bottom Line

The game of investing in bonds is a game of weighing your own expectations about the direction of interest rates against the spread in the market between long and short term rates. The spread was still unusually large at the end of 1985, which tells us that the market expected short rates to rebound upward in 1986. The investor who disagreed and instead felt that short rates were likely to remain stable or decline in 1986 would have been a buyer of long term bonds. If short rates did not rise in 1986 as the market expected, the prices of long term bonds would be bid up as other investors became convinced that bonds offered more attractive yields than had been generally expected. Was your crystal ball clearer than the market's?

2

Inflation, or
How Fast Do I Have to Run
Just to Stand Still?

Imagine that you go to the supermarket once a month with exactly the same shopping list each time and you keep track of how much you spend. Your total grocery bill might fall in June as fresh vegetables become more plentiful. It might rise in January when a snowstorm slows the supply of cattle to market, pushing up the price of beef. However, if your bill rises almost every month, then we say there is *inflation*, a generally pervasive and persistent rise in prices. Unfortunately, this is exactly what we all have experienced during the past 20 years.

The *rate of inflation* is the percentage change in your cash register total over a period of time. Of course, we would like to measure inflation not just at the supermarket, but also at the department store, at the gas pump, and in the housing market. The U.S. Department of Labor does this each month, sampling prices of items in a representative "market basket," and it publishes the resulting Consumer Price Index late the following month. The media always announce the inflation rate as the percent change in the CPI from the prior month, for example, "Inflation rose 0.6 percent in February or 7.2 percent at an annual rate." A much more meaningful indicator of inflation is the percent change from the same month of the prior year. The month-to-month rates are just too noisy to be useful because particular events, such as snowstorms, do distort the CPI temporarily. The year-to-year change has the effect of averaging out these random events, giving a better picture of the underlying trend of prices in the economy. This tells about how much we would have had to increase our investment portfolio and income over the past year just to be standing still in terms of what we can buy.

The rate of inflation measured by the CPI on a year-to-year basis is pictured in Figure 5. It shows that inflation was very low from 1960 through 1965 when it began its frightening upward march to the heights of 1980. Does this picture look rather like the picture of short term interest rates that we saw in Figure 1? It sure does. Coincidental? No, but more about that later.

Notice that the upward march of inflation from 1965 to 1980, though relentless, was not without temporary respite. Some easing occurred in 1967, 1971–1972, and 1975–1976, following recessions in the U.S. economy. As factories and people became unemployed, the upward pressure on prices (and wages) subsided. However, each subsequent peak in inflation was at a higher level, as were the troughs—until 1982. From a hardly noticeable level of 1 percent to 2 percent in the early 1960s, inflation surged to a fever pitch of about 15 percent during 1980—a rate unknown in the United States since the end of World War II. Recently, inflation has subsided to the levels of 20

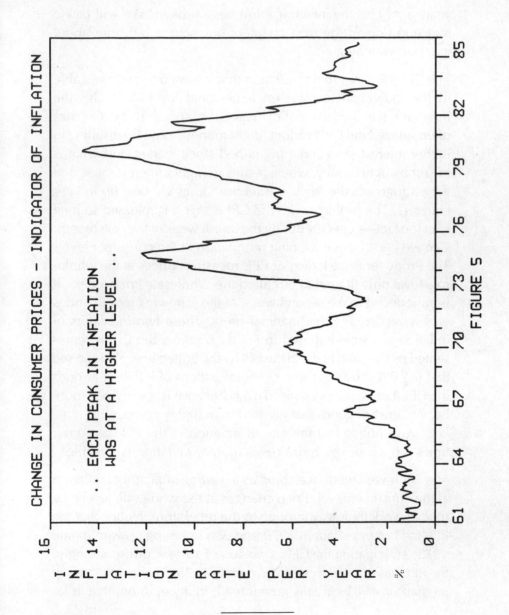

CHANGE IN CONSUMER PRICES - INDICATOR OF INFLATION

.. EACH PEAK IN INFLATION
WAS AT A HIGHER LEVEL ..

FIGURE 5

INFLATION RATE PER YEAR %

years ago. Has the inflation spiral been broken? We will tackle that question in the next chapter, but now a bit more about inflation-watching.

The CPI is the measure of inflation that is most directly applicable to the individual investor on a personal level. It is also the indicator watched by policymakers. A surge in the CPI has often spurred the Fed to adopt "tight money" policies resulting in higher interest rates and a frightened stock market. Just what is meant by tight money, why it results in higher interest rates, and why it frightens the stock market are topics we take up in later chapters. The problem with the CPI is that it is released so long after the fact—generally during the fourth week of the next month. Can we get advance warning of inflation at the consumer level? The Producer Price Index, or PPI, measures prices at the wholesale level only (it used to be called the Wholesale Price Index). It is announced in the second week of the following month and is widely reported in the financial press. These two indicators of inflation are superimposed in Figure 6 where the CPI is represented by the solid line and the PPI by the dotted line. You can see that the PPI shows the same general pattern of inflation as does the CPI, but is more volatile. This is because it is weighted more heavily toward goods that are traded in highly competitive markets. Also notice that the rate of inflation in the PPI has sometimes dipped *below* zero. Yes, Virginia, *deflation* is possible!

The PPI is well worth watching as a *leading indicator* of inflation at the consumer level. Price changes at the wholesale level take time to work their way through to the retail store. Notice that the PPI had bottomed out in 1970 and was zooming upward in late 1972, anticipating the CPI explosion of 1974. Correspondingly, the PPI was quicker to subside in early 1975. The low PPI rate of increase in 1983 virtually guaranteed, in my opinion, that infla-

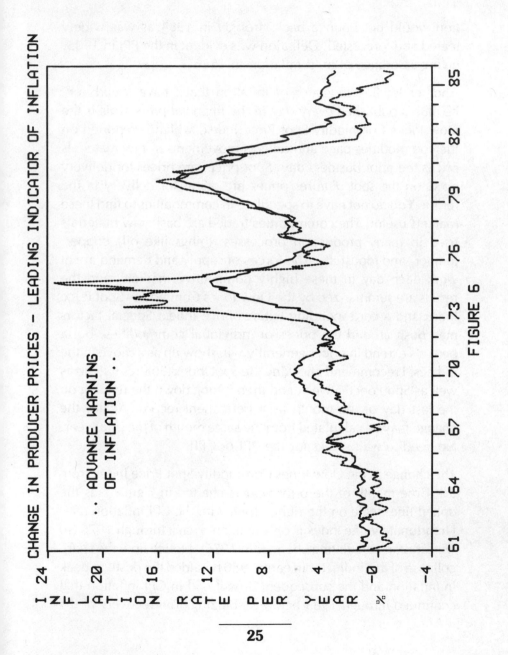

CHANGE IN PRODUCER PRICES - LEADING INDICATOR OF INFLATION

.. ADVANCE WARNING
OF INFLATION ..

INFLATION RATE PER YEAR %

24
20
16
12
8
4
-0
-4

61 64 67 70 73 76 79 82 85

FIGURE 6

25

tion would not bounce back strongly in 1984 as was widely feared and forecasted. Deflation was evident in the PPI in 1985, giving assurance of mild inflation in 1986.

Another leading indicator of inflation that I have found very helpful is published *every day* in the financial press. This is the Dow Jones Commodity Spot Price Index, which is reported on the commodities page and reflects movements in raw materials prices the prior business day. *Spot* prices are prices for delivery now, on the spot. *Futures* prices are prices for delivery in the future. You do not have to speculate in commodities to find these markets useful. The commodities traded are basic raw materials used in many production processes: things like oil, copper, lumber, and foodstuffs. The forces of supply and demand are at work each day in these highly competitive markets, and the results are summarized by the Dow Jones Commodity Spot Price Index and a corresponding Futures Price Index. Special factors may push around the prices of individual commodities, but a pervasive trend in prices generally will show up as a move in the indices. I recommend checking the Spot Index (Futures will do as well as Spot) once a week and then jotting down the reading on the last day of the month as a permanent record. Again, the change may be calculated from the same month of the prior year. No need to wait weeks for the PPI or CPI!

The change in the Dow Jones Commodity Spot Price Index from the same month of the prior year is charted in Figure 7 as the dotted line (scale on the right) along with the CPI inflation rate. Unfortunately, the index is only available back through 1975 (so we can start calculating changes in 1976). Notice how the sharp collapse of this indicator in early 1980 heralded the postwar peak in inflation and the subsequent downtrend in CPI inflation that continued through 1983 before stabilizing. The recovery of the

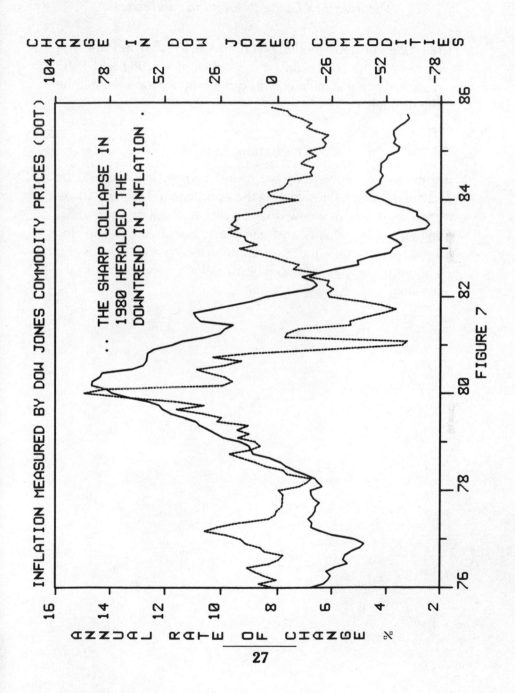

INFLATION MEASURED BY DOW JONES COMMODITY PRICES (DOT)

CHANGE IN DOW JONES COMMODITIES

THE SHARP COLLAPSE IN 1980 HERALDED THE DOWNTREND IN INFLATION .

ANNUAL RATE OF CHANGE %

FIGURE 7

27

1982 recession and a modest pickup in CPI inflation in 1984. The weakness of the commodity price indicator in 1984 and 1985 gave assurance that inflation was quiescent and would continue to be through 1986.

The Bottom Line

In my own experience I have found commodity prices to be particularly helpful in signaling the end of an inflationary surge, or the beginning of a new one. Buying and selling commodity contracts is for experts and gamblers, but investors can find considerable value in the information that commodity prices give us about underlying inflationary (or deflationary!) forces in the economy.

3

Money and the Fed:
Can You Have Too Much
of a Good Thing?

When economists talk about "money" they mean the stuff you use to pay your bills—cash and checking account balances. Money is an asset held for a purpose—to effect transactions. You could offer to trade your stamp collection for groceries, but chances are your local supermarket will insist on money. Generally speaking, it does not make sense to hold money as an investment. Money is a convenience asset rather than an earning asset. H. L. Hunt is reputed to have said that "money is nothing, just something to make the bookkeeping convenient." The word "money" is often given other meanings, and what economists mean when they use the word is a frequent source of confusion in the financial press. For example, if one asks "How much money does the president of General Motors make?" one is inquiring about his income, which is a flow of dollars over a period of time. But when economists talk about the "money supply" they mean the quantity of dollars held in wallets, purses, and bank accounts at a point in time. Bankers sometimes use the word *money* to mean *loan*. Hence "the cost of money" in banker's parlance means the interest rate charged on a loan. Similarly *money market* means *loan market* or *short term securities market*. When a company borrows at the bank or issues commercial paper in the market it certainly receives money, but this cash is quickly disbursed to pay for things the firm needs to buy, such as machines or inventory.

Money is like a hot potato; it gets passed around, but *someone* is holding it. If I have more money than I need to meet current bills, I can convert it to earning assets or things that I can use. However, if everyone has more money on hand than he or she needs, then we get inflation. This is because excess money will chase assets and goods until prices are bid up enough to the point where the existing quantity of money is needed for transactions purposes. This may seem paradoxical—how could we ever have too much money? Here is a fairy tale about money:

The Christmas Fable of Good King Simple VIII

Knowing that his subjects worked hard for their money, well-meaning King Simple VIII decided to send each of his subjects a parcel of money for Christmas. He had the Royal Mint print enough extra pieces of paper with his picture on them to double the number of dollar bills in each subject's pocket. The extra dollars were packaged and mailed in individual parcels to each subject. King Simple knew that receiving the parcel would make his subjects very happy. Of course the parcels did make each subject happy, until he or she tried to spend the contents. *Everyone* now had more cash in hand than was needed to effect transactions, and all these people were trying to convert their Christmas present into something useful. Mr. Jones paid his Christmas money to Mr. Smith for a partridge, but now Mr. Jones's extra dollars were in Mr. Smith's pocket, and he hoped to buy two partridges. But the number of partridges for sale in the kingdom had not changed. The new dollars went from one hand to the next like a hot potato as the prices of partridges, pear trees, land, bread, and everything else started to rise. After all, the quantity of things people wanted was the same as before—only the dollars available to try to buy them had changed. Prices rose until Mr. Jones and Mr. Smith and everyone else found they *needed* the doubled amount of money now in their pockets to effect normal transactions. This happened when prices of nearly everything had about doubled. There were twice as many pictures of the King in people's pockets, but twice as many were needed for each trip to the market square. Even Good King Simple could see now that printing money causes inflation!

A bit silly, yes, but not terribly unrealistic. In fact, the King Simples of today live in Washington, D.C., and other world capitals. The details are a bit more complicated though. Instead of the King's mint we have a Federal Reserve Board, affectionately known as "the Fed." This is an independent government agency (not privately owned), run by a Board of Governors, with the power and authority to create money. How? By buying U.S. Treasury bills or bonds on the open market with money that did not exist before. Specifically, the Fed purchases the securities from a bank and pays the bank by crediting the bank's account at the Fed for the agreed amount. The Fed is the bank's bank. The bank can then draw on this balance to make loans to its customers. Mrs. Jones might borrow some of it to pay for a new roof on her house. The roofer deposits the money at his bank and then disperses it to pay his bills. This is the process by which the new money circulates around the banking system from account to account. It cannot be used up or disappear. It just changes hands. It is like the hot potato.

How do we measure money? Banks and other institutions offering checkable accounts are required to report their liabilities to depositors, and this gives the Fed a reading on the total amount of cash and checking balances in the system, which together is called the "money supply." The announcement of the money supply figures on Thursday afternoon is a weekly event on Wall Street, and its approach engenders much fear and trepidation. An unexpected rise can push the stock and bond markets down sharply. Why so nervous? The answer lies in the sorry record of monetary mismanagement that led to drastic changes in the Fed's policy in October 1979.

To see where we have come from, look at Figure 8, which shows the percentage rate of change in the money supply—the "M2" measure—from the corresponding month of the prior year. Weekly numbers, so eagerly anticipated on Wall Street, are too noisy to be very useful. What is announced weekly is "M1," a "narrow" measure of money limited to currency and checkable deposits. M2 is announced monthly and includes money market mutual fund assets and similar accounts at banks in addition to M1. Notice that relatively stable money growth gave way in the late 1960s to a series of ever-wilder gyrations—a plunge in 1966, a new peak in 1967–1968 followed by an even sharper plunge in 1969–1970. Then 1972 saw money growth reach new heights—

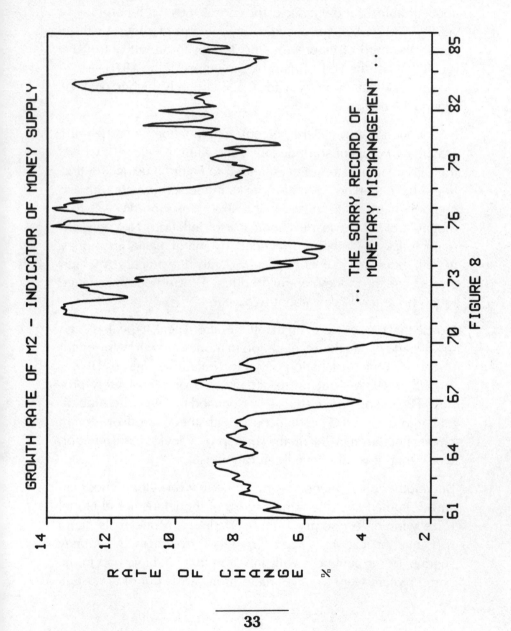

GROWTH RATE OF M2 – INDICATOR OF MONEY SUPPLY

.. THE SORRY RECORD OF
MONETARY MISMANAGEMENT ..

FIGURE 8

about double the growth rate of the early 1960s. The energy crisis years, 1974−1975, produced a new dive in money growth to about one third of its previous peak. Not to be left out of the record books, the Fed's Board of Governors of the 1976−1977 period took money growth to a new, slightly higher peak of around 14 percent.

Now if money grows at 14 percent, can inflation be far behind? Maybe two years or so! Judge for yourself from Figure 9, where the CPI inflation rate has been added to Figure 8 using a dotted line. I have marked the major peaks in money growth with a *P* and drawn arrows to subsequent peaks in inflation. We see that money growth is a *leading indicator* of inflation. Not only are major peaks in inflation preceded by major peaks in money growth, but so are major troughs. Evidently, the process by which a change in the money supply produces a corresponding change in the price level takes about two years.

Notice that the acceleration in inflation from peak to peak is even more marked than the acceleration in money growth. Why might this be so? One explanation is that the inflation surges of 1974− 1975 and 1979−1980 were accentuated or even largely produced by the oil "price shocks" associated first with the Arab oil embargo and OPEC, and second, with the shut-off of Iranian crude after the fall of the Shah. These price shocks made inflation worse than it would have been otherwise.

But another phenomenon seems to be at work—the "Friedman surge" named after the famous guru of monetarism and Nobel Prize winning economist Milton Friedman. Monetarists claim that inflation can be traced largely to growth in the money supply. The experiences with inflation that we have had in the past 25 years seem to have made monetarists out of almost all

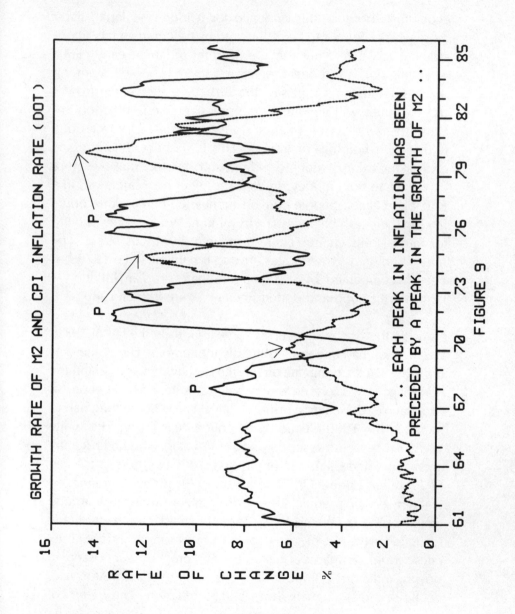

GROWTH RATE OF M2 AND CPI INFLATION RATE (DOT)

.. EACH PEAK IN INFLATION HAS BEEN
PRECEDED BY A PEAK IN THE GROWTH OF M2 ..

FIGURE 9

35

economists because the evidence for it looms so large. Even those who claim not to be influenced by monetarism talk about inflation very differently from the way they did in the early 1960s when inflation was thought to emanate from U.S. Steel's pricing policies. Friedman's surge says that an acceleration of the growth rate of money will yield a disproportionate rise in inflation because the very fact of inflation causes people to try to reduce further their holdings of money. This is because inflation eats away at the value of money holdings and therefore makes it more expensive to hold money. In countries with hyperinflation, like Brazil and Israel, people convert money to goods within hours to keep their cash balances at a minimum. When money growth is reduced, this vicious circle turns into a virtuous circle. The return to money growth rates around 8 percent since 1979 has been accompanied by a disproportionate drop in inflation—compare the solid and dotted lines in Figure 9 after 1980.

How did this dramatic reversal come about? By the fall of 1979, the situation had become politically intolerable. The dollar was dropping at a dizzying rate on foreign exchange markets, and the price of gold was soaring to new heights. Inflation had become a national obsession and a prime political issue. Something had to be done; the 1980 election was only a year away. The white knight riding to our rescue was Paul Volcker, who had recently been appointed Chairman of the Board of Governors of the Fed by President Carter. On October 6, 1979, the Fed announced that henceforth it would set strict targets for money growth and would abide by them. These targets would require a steady reduction in the rate of growth of the money supply and the target rates would be made public. Has this program succeeded in slowing inflation? Without a doubt. Is inflation beaten? As long as public sentiment remains opposed to inflation. The means of controlling it are no mystery. The present generation of Americans has experienced real inflation, and few would care to see it repeated.

The nervousness of the financial markets every Thursday afternoon is a testimony to the credibility which the Fed and Mr. Volcker have achieved since October 1979. Investors know that if the money supply grows too fast the Fed will take action to reduce it. How does the Fed reduce the money supply? It reverses the process described earlier for creating money. The Fed simply sells securities from its portfolio on the open market. When it receives payment from the buyer, that amount of money has been withdrawn from the banking system. Of course, a large sale of U.S. Treasury securities by the Fed tends to push down the prices of all securities in the marketplace including stocks. Little wonder then that Thursday afternoons are a nervous time of the week on Wall Street.

But wait, you say, what about the sharp peak in the growth of M2 during 1983 which shows up in Figures 8 and 9? Isn't this the harbinger of a new bout of double-digit inflation in 1985? That's precisely what a number of prominent monetarists proclaimed at the time, but 1985 came and went without any sign that inflation was making a comeback. Why didn't it? Recall that 1983 was the first year that banks all over the country started offering checking accounts that paid interest—called "NOW" or SUPERNOW" accounts or "market interest" accounts. Congress felt that they had to give the banks and S&L's the capability to compete with money market mutual funds which had been paying market interest on checkable accounts since the early 1970s. Depositors moved quickly to take advantage of these new bank accounts, but were obliged to increase their minimum balance to $2500 or even $5000. These new accounts are included in M2, and much of the funds that went into them came from maturing CDs that are not part of M2. This produced a temporary explosion of money growth, but not one which indicated an accumulation of excess balances waiting to be spent. It represented a change in the *demand* for money and the Fed increased the *supply* of money to meet it. The underlying more modest and noninflationary growth rate of M2 was evident again during 1985.

What can investors do during a time when monetary indicators become unreliable because of major restrictions in the banking system? My strategy has been to rely more heavily on other indicators of inflationary pressure, such as the commodity price indices and PPI, as well as indicators we will discuss in later chapters.

The Bottom Line

Money is the stuff we use to pay our bills: cash and checking accounts. The amount of it, the money supply, is controlled by the Federal Reserve. When there is more of it than we need to carry out transactions, then inflation is the result. Deregulation of banks, and savings and loans has made the money supply numbers harder to interpret in the 1980s, so investors should keep a close eye on commodity prices and the PPI for signs of renewed inflation.

4

Have Interest Rates
Been High, Really?

If rapid growth of the money supply causes inflation, what does inflation cause? Besides ulcers, it causes high interest rates. Investors are concerned with what they *really* earn on their savings, and what they really earn is the rate of return in dollars *minus* the rate of inflation. For example, if I earn 10 percent over a year's time on my money market fund but inflation has been running at a rate of 10 percent, then I have not really earned anything on my investment. The number of dollars I have at the end of the year is 10 percent greater, but it has no more buying power than did my original investment. The *real rate of return* or *real interest rate* is the dollar rate of return minus the inflation rate. This is also the real interest cost to a borrower. The willingness of lenders to lend and borrowers to borrow should depend on the *real rate of interest* rather than on the dollar or *nominal* rate of interest. Is 14 percent a high rate of interest to earn or to pay? The answer really depends on what the inflation rate is going to be.

It seems reasonable that real interest rates would be fairly stable over long periods of time because the willingness of lenders to lend and borrowers to borrow is unlikely to change a great deal. If the real rate is stable then a rise in inflation *must* result in higher nominal interest rates. It must, but has it really? Consider Figure 10, in which we have superimposed the yield on three-month Treasury bills (from Figure 1) and the CPI inflation rate (from Figure 5) for 1961 through 1985. The two track each other closely but not perfectly. Most of the time the interest rate is above inflation, meaning that the real rate of return was positive. Notice though that Treasury bills failed to offer a positive real return during the 1974–1975 period of rapid post-OPEC inflation and recession. They offered a large positive real return during the 1981–1984 period—interest rates were falling, but not as fast as inflation was falling. To see the behavior of the real interest rate

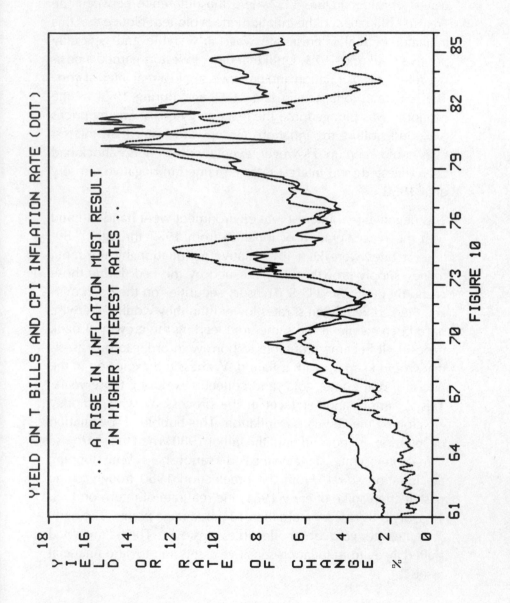

YIELD ON T BILLS AND CPI INFLATION RATE (DOT)

... A RISE IN INFLATION MUST RESULT
IN HIGHER INTEREST RATES ..

FIGURE 10

better, consider Figure 11, where the difference between the Treasury bill rate and the inflation rate is plotted. Notice that this indicator of real interest rate was fairly stable and generally positive until mid-1973. Until that date, investors earned a positive return net of inflation and borrowers paid a real interest cost. The real rate collapsed in late 1973 and during 1974 as the economy was plunged into the first energy crisis. Energy prices exploded, jolting the inflation rate upward faster than interest rates could keep up. However, even after the energy shock had been digested, real interest rates remained in negative territory until 1980.

This negative real interest rate environment went hand-in-hand with the reacceleration of inflation from 1977 through 1980. Interest rates were kept low relative to inflation by the rapid money supply growth policy pursued by the Fed during those years. By purchasing U.S. Treasury securities on the open market, the Fed kept interest rates lower than they would otherwise have been, while at the same time feeding the growth of bank deposits. It became profitable to borrow in order to buy assets that would keep up with inflation. Witness the explosion in the prices of real estate, gold, and collectibles during those years. This is simply another facet of the process by which money creation by the Fed causes inflation. This bubble of speculation on inflation did not end until the fall of 1980 when the sharp rise in real interest rates signaled the Fed's seriousness about stopping the inflation spiral. From the preelection 1980 trough to the postelection spike of early 1981, the real rate of return on U.S. Treasury bills rose by more than 13 percentage points! The party in real estate, gold, and collectibles was over. The balance had shifted away from inflation-sensitive assets and toward financial assets.

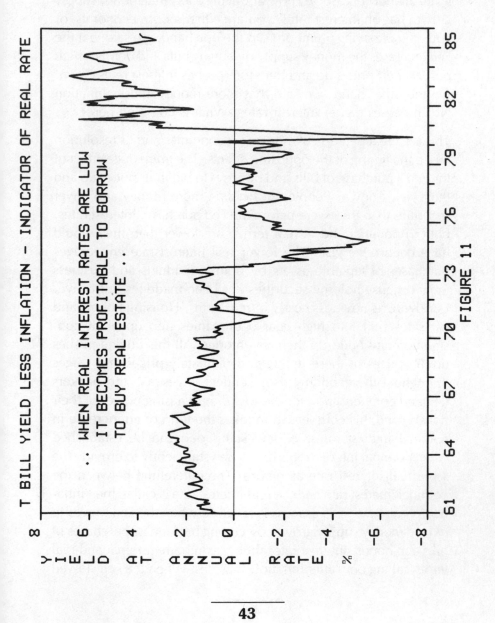

T BILL YIELD LESS INFLATION - INDICATOR OF REAL RATE

.. WHEN REAL INTEREST RATES ARE LOW
IT BECOMES PROFITABLE TO BORROW
TO BUY REAL ESTATE ..

FIGURE 11

YIELD AT ANNUAL RATE %

If you are not confused by now about the effect that money supply growth has on interest rates, you are either a born economist or you are not paying attention! On the one hand, we said that the Fed increases the money supply by buying bills and bonds which pushes their prices up and therefore pushes interest rates down. On the other hand, we said that more money causes inflation which causes *higher* interest rates. What is going on here?

This is a great paradox of monetary economics and its resolution lies in the timing of the opposing effects. The *immediate* effect of the Fed's purchase of bills and bonds *is* to bid their prices up and their yields down. People are holding more money and fewer securities than they were before the Fed purchase. Interest rates, both in nominal and in real terms, are lower than they would have been otherwise. The lower real interest rate encourages purchases of tangible assets by both individuals and business firms because holding securities has been made less attractive. Borrowing is now less costly in real terms. Housing booms and car sales shift into high gear. Companies step up plant construction and build up their inventories. All this buying pushes up the prices of these items, and ultimately prices and wages throughout the economy rise. Lenders, investors, and bankers demand compensation for the loss of purchasing power of their dollars, and this compensation takes the form of an increase in nominal interest rates. A new status quo can be established when nominal interest rates have risen sufficiently to provide the same real interest rate as before. The differential between the nominal interest rate and the real interest rate is called the "inflation premium." This process is reversed when the Fed moves to reduce money supply growth by cutting back on its purchases of bills and bonds. Interest rates then rise in both nominal and real terms, falling only after inflation subsides. When the Fed slowed money growth in the early 1980s it pushed interest rates higher, but this paved the way for lower interest rates in the mid-1980s. That is the paradox of monetary economics.

This distinction between the immediate effect of money growth on interest rates and the longer term effect is clearly evident in Figure 12 where the Treasury bill yield is the solid line and M2 money growth is the dotted line. Sharp accelerations in money growth generally coincide with interest rate troughs, only to be followed by high interest rates. Sharp slowdowns in money growth precede interest rate peaks, followed subsequently by lower interest rates. The "disinflation" which began with the tight money policy of the Fed in 1979 finally bore fruit in the securities markets in 1982 when nominal interest rates dropped significantly. Although rates backed up a bit in mid-1984, the general trend in interest rates followed the trend of inflation downward through 1985.

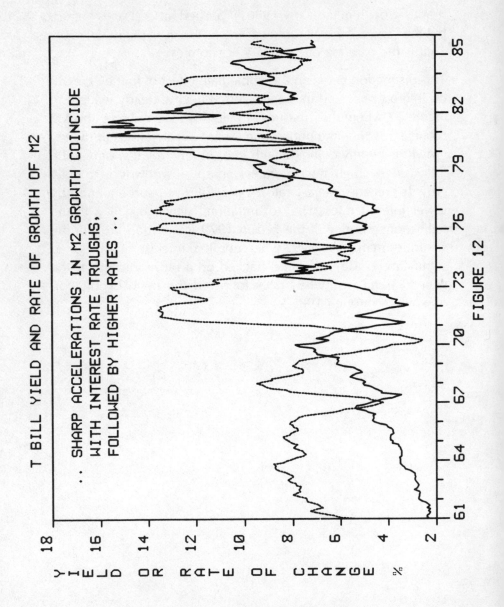

T BILL YIELD AND RATE OF GROWTH OF M2

.. SHARP ACCELERATIONS IN M2 GROWTH COINCIDE
WITH INTEREST RATE TROUGHS,
FOLLOWED BY HIGHER RATES ..

FIGURE 12

YIELD OR RATE OF CHANGE %

Have Interest Rates Been High, Really?

The Bottom Line

Higher inflation means higher interest rates because lenders demand compensation for the loss of the buying power of their dollars and borrowers find they can afford to pay it. The difference between the stated or nominal interest rate and the rate of inflation is called the *real interest rate*. The decline in interest rates after 1982 was largely due to the decline of inflation; real interest rates remained relatively high.

5

The Stock Market:
Refuge from Inflation or Trap?

There were few more cherished articles of faith on Wall Street in the 1960s than the one which said that the value of stocks would rise in line with general inflation—and none that have been more rudely shattered. The logic of this credo was simple: The prices of the goods produced by a corporation would rise by the amount of the inflation and, consequently, so would its profits and its dividend payments to stockholders. Stocks therefore offered a refuge, a hedge against inflation. An investment in stocks would not lose its purchasing power if inflation heated up—its market value would just grow at the rate of inflation. Impeccable logic—but dead wrong.

The best indicator of stock market value I know of is the Standard & Poor's 500 Stock Index, which is pictured in Figure 13. The S & P 500 not only includes many more stocks than the popular Dow Jones Industrial Average, it is a value-weighted index, which

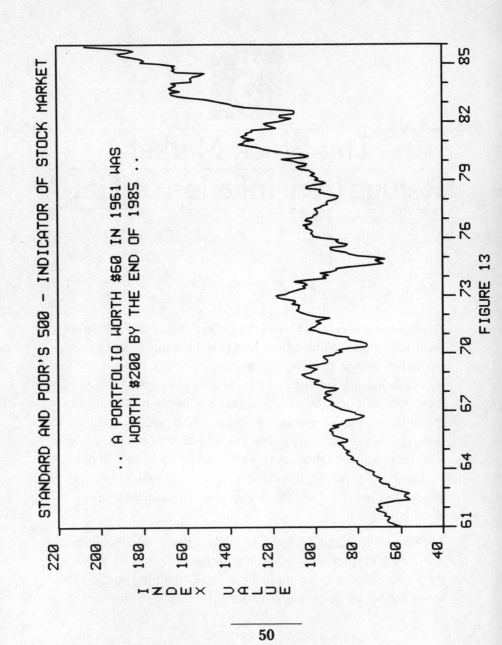

STANDARD AND POOR'S 500 - INDICATOR OF STOCK MARKET

... A PORTFOLIO WORTH $60 IN 1961 WAS
WORTH $200 BY THE END OF 1985 ...

FIGURE 13

INDEX VALUE

50

means that it is a more realistic indicator of what has happened to the value of representative stock portfolios. It is published daily in *The Wall Street Journal* and many local newspapers. Figure 13 shows that a broadly based portfolio of common stocks that was worth $60 in 1961 was worth over $100 in 1968, then slumped to only about $70 in 1974, surged to $135 in 1980, and finished 1985 at about $207. With all of the ups and downs, this market portfolio grew at a rate of over 5 percent per year compounded. Not a bad performance—or is it, really?

In order to assess the *real* performance of the stock market we need to compare stock values with the cost of living, which also rose a great deal during that period. According to the CPI, the cost of a representative basket of consumer goods that was $89 in 1961, rose to $104 in 1968, to $145 in 1974, to $250 by 1980, and to about $327 by the end of 1985! Obviously, the stock market failed to protect the typical investor from inflation, because the cost of living rose faster than the value of stocks.

If we divide the stock market index by the cost of living index we get an indicator of the *real value* or *purchasing power* of stock market portfolios. Using the S & P 500 Index and the CPI to calculate this ratio, we get the indicator of real stock market value charted in Figure 14. Since the CPI has the value 100 in 1967 (its base year) we can think of this as the value of stocks in terms of 1967 dollars. What a different picture of stock market performance it presents! The indicator rose from $.67 in 1961 to about $.96 in 1968, since stock prices rose faster than the cost of living. But the real value of stocks slumped sharply in the energy crisis of 1974 to about $.48. Although the stock market rose between 1974 and 1980, the cost of living rose almost as fast, so the real value indicator only inched up to $.54. Then came the 1981–1982 bear market and by mid-1982 it had fallen to a mere $.37!

51

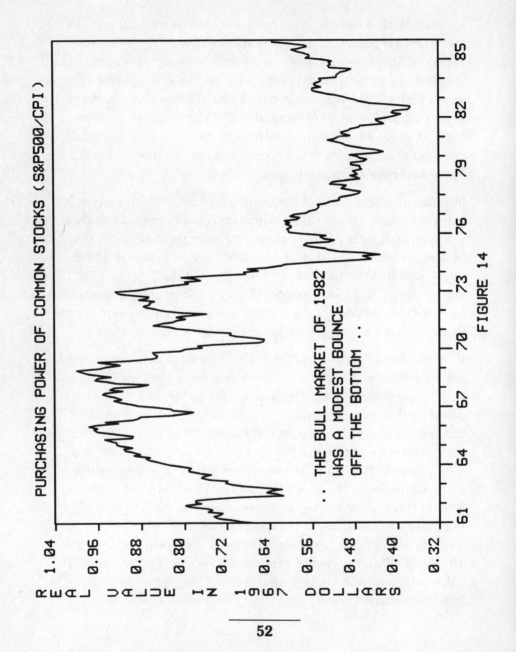

PURCHASING POWER OF COMMON STOCKS (S&P500/CPI)

.. THE BULL MARKET OF 1982
WAS A MODEST BOUNCE
OFF THE BOTTOM ..

FIGURE 14

The Stock Market: Refuge from Inflation or Trap?

In this perspective, the bull market of August 1982—July 1983 is just a bounce off the floor! By the end of 1985, the real value of stocks was back up to $.63—a big improvement but well below the high plateau of the 1963—1972 period when it was around the $.90 level.

I must confess that the first time I saw this chart of real stock market value I thought that some error must have been made in the calculations. I simply didn't realize that investors had been that badly savaged in the 1973—1982 decade. From the peak in January 1973 to the trough in July 1982, the real loss in the S & P 500 portfolio was a staggering 60 percent! Only half of this loss had been recovered by the end of 1985—so the upside potential for *real* appreciation in stock market values is still very large.

Let's take a closer look at how the stock market responded to inflation by superimposing Figure 5, inflation measured by CPI, and Figure 13, the S & P 500 Index. The resulting picture in Figure 15 shows that the stock market not only provided no protection from inflation, it retreated in the face of it! As inflation accelerated in 1966, the stock market fell sharply. It recovered when inflation subsided in the new year. As the inflation moved up again in the late 1960s, the market topped in 1968, and then plunged. The easing of inflation in the early 1970s was accompanied by a major bull market. This bull market peaked out in early 1973 after inflation had again started to accelerate. The stock market continued its plunge until inflation peaked at the end of 1974. Some of you commodity-watchers will recall that commodity prices broke in October 1974, heralding the end of the first OPEC inflation shock. The stock market bottomed out two months later. The next stock market peak coincided with another inflation trough at the end of 1976. During the big acceleration of inflation from 1977 through 1979 the stock market basically

53

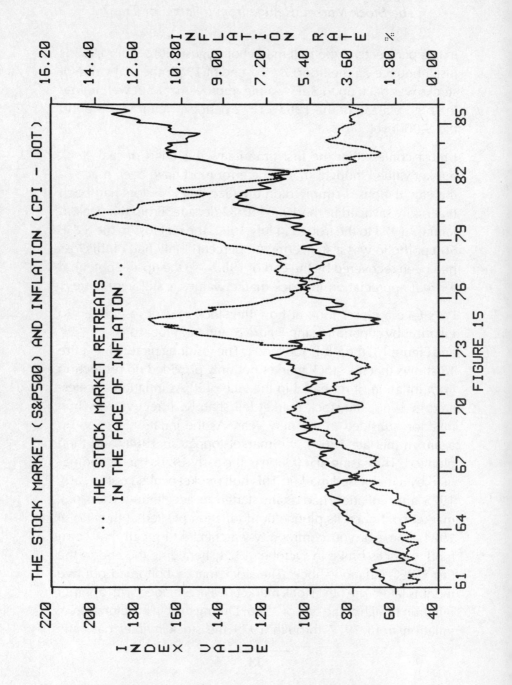

THE STOCK MARKET (S&P500) AND INFLATION (CPI – DOT)

... THE STOCK MARKET RETREATS
IN THE FACE OF INFLATION ...

FIGURE 15

moved sideways, but investors were suffering a considerable loss of purchasing power (see Figure 14). The market didn't really make sustained forward progress until 1982 when inflation had dropped back to the levels of the 1960s. With continued moderate inflation the stock market then doubled by the end of 1985. If it seems to you that inflation might have some potential as an indicator of the future direction of the stock market, I agree and we will look into this possibility in Chapter 12.

Why did the stock market fail investors so badly as an inflation hedge? Where did the simple logic behind Wall Street's 1960s credo go wrong? This is the subject of the next chapter.

The Bottom Line

Contrary to traditional Wall Street wisdom, inflation proved to be a disaster for the stock market. The purchasing power of representative stock portfolios fell by about 60 percent in the inflation-ridden 1973–1982 decade. The stock market rallied in 1982 only after inflation had subsided to the levels of the 1960s. When inflation heats up again, the prudent investor will beat a hasty retreat to the money market funds.

6

The Real Economy

The purchasing power of a society is limited to what it produces—a simple and obvious fact, but one that is often ignored by politicians like our friend King Simple VIII. The *real income* of a society is the quantity of goods and services it produces. This production takes place in what I call the *real economy*—factories, mines, transportation systems, stores, hospitals, and service outlets. The income from these activities is distributed to employees, suppliers, and creditors, with the remainder being the earnings accruing to stockholders as the owners of business firms. Although the distribution of income takes place in the form of dollars, the purchasing power of this income across society cannot exceed what has been produced. No government program can enhance economic welfare unless it strengthens the real economy. What this tells us is that the real income of shareholders (indeed, of everyone) is directly linked to the performance of the real economy. In particular, we will see that the poor performance of the stock market in real terms from the late 1960s through the early 1980s went hand-in-hand with poor performance in the real economy.

The most widely publicized indicator of the real economy is the GNP, which stands for Gross National Product. It may well be the best-known acronym of all. The newly released GNP figures receive headline status in the press and are announced on TV in the tone reserved for matters of great import by evening network anchorpersons. A rise in the latest number is taken to be cause for rejoicing and any reduction as a development of the greatest gravity. It is doubtful that any statistic of any sort has ever been treated with more respect or imbued with more significance than is the GNP. The Nobel Prize in economics was awarded to Professor Simon Kuznets of Harvard University for inventing it. Does it warrant all the ballyhoo?

GNP is designed to measure the total value of all goods and services produced in the economy. It encompasses the activities of private business, nonprofit institutions, and governments. Precisely because it is all-encompassing in its scope, there are serious conceptual problems in its design and practical problems in collecting and assembling all the data that go into it. Let's stop and think for a minute what is involved. To measure the value of goods produced by Procter & Gamble, we only need to find out the company's sales and subtract from that the cost of raw materials used. The result is the *value added* by Procter & Gamble in turning those raw materials into goods purchased by consumers. We understand *value* here to mean *market value*. But what is the value of government? What is the value of a public university? Neither sells its services in a market. What is the value of the services produced in a hospital? The GNP accountants get around these conceptual problems by assuming that the *value* of what's produced in governmental and nonprofit organizations is simply equal to the *cost*, since costs are readily measured. Some important economic activities do not get counted in GNP at all. For example, no value is placed on production in the household. When more families become two-income families, GNP rises automatically. Dinner at McDonald's contributes to official GNP, dinner at home (no matter how well prepared) does not.

In addition to formidable conceptual problems in measuring GNP, there are many practical ones. The sheer complexity of the economy means that a great deal of "guesstimation" goes into the numbers based on very incomplete information, and it all takes quite a while to assemble. Because of the size of the job, GNP is measured only on a quarterly basis. During the third week of the month following a calendar quarter, the U.S. Department of Commerce releases preliminary GNP figures for that quarter. For example, in the third week of January 1985, we heard that—

The U.S. economy grew at a healthy 3.9% inflation adjusted annual rate in the last quarter of 1984.

Now that was pretty good news. It indicated that the real economy, as measured by real GNP, was growing at a pace that was somewhat above the average growth rate since World War II. Unfortunately, not all the returns were in on that final quarter of 1984. That 3.9 percent rate of growth was only an estimate. After more data became available the GNP accountants revised their estimates downward and a year later the official result was that the U.S. economy had actually grown at only a sluggish 0.6 percent rate in the fourth quarter of 1984. If the GNP numbers had given us an accurate reading back in January 1985, then perhaps the lackluster growth rate of the real economy in 1985 would have come as less of a surprise.

The sad fact is that GNP fails the timely release criterion for useful economic indicators. It is also weak on the criterion of relevance to investors, since it includes many sectors of the economy in which there is no private investment.

Nevertheless, let's take a look at the record of GNP since 1960 in Figure 16, since it does give us an historical picture of the real economy. Notice that GNP is measured in billions of 1982 dollars. What does that mean? The idea is to measure the value of goods and services at the prices which prevailed in 1982. Any change in GNP is then a *real* change and not due to rising prices. An illustration may help. Say that Freeboard Boat Company contributed $100 million of value added to GNP in 1982. In 1983, its value added was $120 million, but the prices of its boats rose on average by 10 percent. In terms of 1982 dollars, its 1983 contribution to GNP is then $110 million, the other $10 million (10 percent of $100 million) having been due to inflation. When we add all these contributions up across the economy, we get *real* GNP. If no adjustment is made for price change, we would be measuring what is called *nominal GNP*. Real GNP is sometimes called "GNP in constant dollars," and nominal GNP is sometimes called "GNP in current dollars." It is the real GNP that is reported in the media because people want to know how the economy is doing in real terms—whether the sum total of cars, refrigerators, boats, haircuts, appendectomies, tax audits, and everything else produced by the economy has increased or decreased. The discrepancy between growth in nominal GNP and growth in real GNP is a measure of how much inflation there has been. This measure is called the "implicit price deflator" or "the GNP measure of inflation."

But getting back to our Figure 16, what does it tell us about the real economy? Notice that there have been five dips in the real

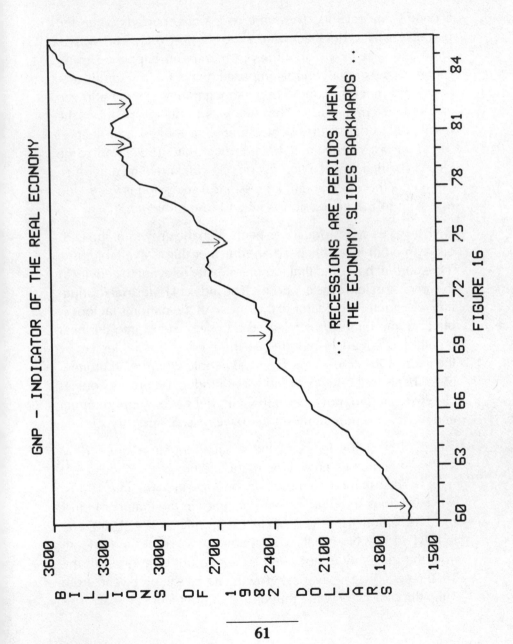

GNP — INDICATOR OF THE REAL ECONOMY

.. RECESSIONS ARE PERIODS WHEN
THE ECONOMY SLIDES BACKWARDS ..

FIGURE 16

economy since 1960. These are *recessions*, periods when the real economy slides backward. The shortest recession was in 1980 and lasted only about seven months. It happened in response to the credit controls imposed by the Carter Administration. Remember that one? People thought they weren't allowed to use their credit cards. The idea was to defeat inflation; the result was to defeat President Carter. The longest and deepest recession lasted from mid-1981 through late 1982, and came close to being labeled a *depression*. Do you know the difference between a recession and a depression? A recession is when you lose your job, a depression is when I lose mine!

GNP gives us an historical perspective on the growth of the U.S. economy, but investors need an indicator that is available on a more current basis and that is more directly relevant to activity in the private sector of the economy. The Index of Industrial Production is a monthly indicator of the output of the nation's factories, utilities, and mines. It is released only two weeks into the next month and is widely reported in the media. It is collected by the Federal Reserve—yes, the same people who create money. Movements in the Index of Industrial Production are, of course, closely related to movements in GNP, but give us a more direct and more current reading on the pace of U.S. industry.

The picture of the Index of Industrial Production since 1960 shown in Figure 17 gives a dramatic picture of the shocks that have been sustained by the real economy since the late 1960s. The recessions show up as sharp declines in the Index of Industrial Production. This occurred in 1960, 1970, 1974, 1980, and in 1981–1982. Note that growth in output was rapid and smooth from the relatively minor 1960 recession until the onset of the 1970 recession. The average growth rate for the nine years from 1961 through 1969 was a thundering 6.4 percent per year com-

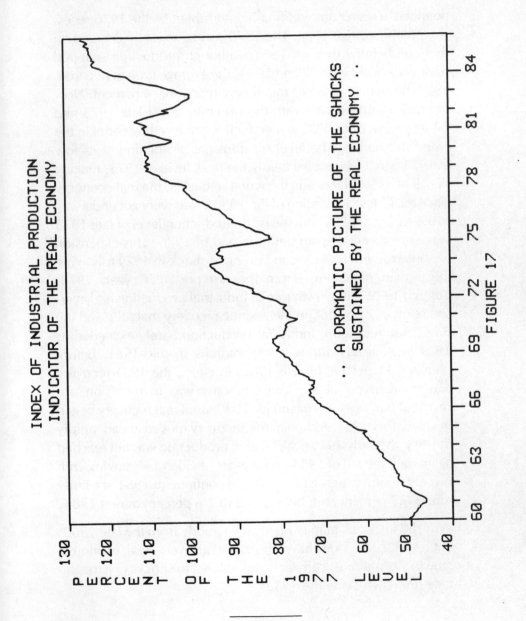

INDEX OF INDUSTRIAL PRODUCTION
INDICATOR OF THE REAL ECONOMY

.. A DRAMATIC PICTURE OF THE SHOCKS
SUSTAINED BY THE REAL ECONOMY ..

FIGURE 17

pounded! This record was finally interrupted by the 1970 recession, the first since 1960. The 1970 recession really dragged on (but unofficially) through 1971. Although production snapped back vigorously in 1972 and 1973, the average growth rate from 1969 through 1973 was a much less impressive 4 percent. Now the real trouble started with the oil embargo of late 1973 and the emergence of OPEC as an effective price-setting cartel in the world oil market. The level of industrial production at its low in 1975 was 14.7 percent *below* the peak level of 1973, making the 1974–1975 recession the worst setback to the real economy since the Great Depression of the 1930s. Recovery got underway in the spring of 1975, but the peak production level of late 1973 was not exceeded again until the end of 1976. This expansion was interrupted by the second oil price shock in 1979 following the Iranian revolution. From the last pre-OPEC year, 1973, through 1979, the growth rate of industrial production had averaged only 2.7 percent. In the anemic recovery that followed the brief 1980 recession, industrial production barely exceeded its 1979 peak levels during a few months in mid-1981, before plunging 11 percent by late 1982. In effect, the 1981 recovery was no recovery at all. The economy was in recession, for practical purposes, from January 1980, until real recovery began in November 1982. Although the recovery moved ahead rapidly in 1983, the early 1979 peak level of production was not reached again until the fall of 1983—four years of violent seesawing with no net forward progress! Growth did continue in 1984 at a fairly robust 6.7 percent rate, but slowed to 2.6 percent during 1985.

Why did the stock market perform so poorly from the late 1960s until 1982? We now have the basic answer: Real economic growth slowed drastically and was subject to shocks of a magnitude unknown since the 1930s.

The Real Economy

Another way to view the performance of the real economy is to look at industrial production relative to the production capacity of the industrial sector. When the Federal Reserve collects the production data from firms that it uses to construct the Index, it also estimates what their full-capacity production level would be. The actual production level as a percent of this full capacity level is called the Rate of Capacity Utilization. It is announced in the media every month, one day after the Index of Industrial Production. This monthly indicator is limited to manufacturing industries, however. The picture it gives of the real economy is shown in Figure 18. From a peak of about 92 percent in 1966, the Rate of Capacity Utilization in U.S. manufacturing has been on a downhill course. After staying above 80 percent for the entire 1962–1969 period, it has since dipped to below 70 percent twice and has been below 80 percent about as many months as it has been above 80 percent. The 1984 rate was only about 81 percent in spite of the much ballyhooed 1983–1984 expansion, and capacity utilization slipped slightly in 1985. More corporate plant and equipment was idle for longer periods as we moved from the 1960s to the 1970s and then to the 1980s. Little wonder that the real value of the stocks representing ownership of those industrial assets was marked down sharply by stock traders.

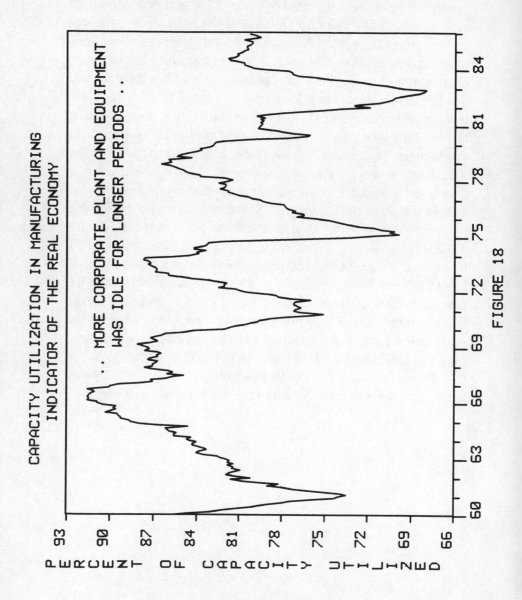

CAPACITY UTILIZATION IN MANUFACTURING
INDICATOR OF THE REAL ECONOMY

.. MORE CORPORATE PLANT AND EQUIPMENT
WAS IDLE FOR LONGER PERIODS ..

FIGURE 18

PERCENT OF CAPACITY UTILIZED

The Real Economy

The Bottom Line

The real economy is the production of things and services. Its measure is known by the best known acronym of all: GNP. A more useful indicator of the economy for investors is the Index of Industrial Production because it's more current. The performance of the real economy has been poorer since the early 1970s—recessions have been more severe, overall growth has been slower, and more of the productive capacity of industry has been idle. Stocks are shares in the real economy, and their value reflects its performance—excellent in the 1960s, uneven in the 1973–1982 decade, improving in the mid-1980s.

7

Profits, Real Profits, and Really Real Profits

Profits are the lifeblood of the stock market. A corporation's shareholders are its owners. They are entitled to whatever is left over after the company has paid its expenses, and that is what profit is. If there were no profits the shares would be worthless. Some of the profit will usually be paid out in cash to the shareholders in the form of dividends, and the rest of it will be reinvested in the business, hopefully resulting in additional profits in the future. In periods of rising profits, investors will bid up the price of the company's shares in anticipation of receiving a higher dividend.

Shares in a company or corporation are referred to as its *stock*. Each share of stock is entitled to an equal portion of the company's profit, an equal dividend, and an equal vote in the election of directors and other matters. To accommodate investors with different tolerances for risk, there are two kinds of stock. *Pre-*

ferred stock, which pays a fixed dividend, is really a debt of the company because it is obliged to pay the preferred dividend before paying any other dividend. Investors who buy preferred stock like the security, but will never receive anything more than the fixed dividend regardless of how well the company does. Shares in the ownership of the company which are not preferred shares are technically known as *common stock*. When investors talk about "stock," though, they almost always mean common stock.

In some circles "profit" is a dirty word, and some investors may prefer to use the nicer-sounding word "earnings." Either way, profits or earnings are what investors get in return for risking their savings to provide the capital needed to buy machines, buildings, and the other things that make possible the production and distribution of goods and the provision of services. Profits depend very directly on the real economy. When production and sales turn down, profits drop even more sharply. This is because many of the expenses of a company go right on regardless of whether business is good or bad. Buildings and equipment continue to depreciate, interest has to be paid on bank loans and bonds, and you can't turn off the heat in the middle of winter. The poor performance of the real economy from the late 1960s through the early 1980s created an environment in which profits simply could not grow. The shocking fact is that profits, adjusted for the effects of inflation, were no higher at the end of 1983 than they were at the end of 1965. They finally rose to a new high in 1984 and continued to soar in 1985. Little wonder then that the stock market stagnated from the late 1960s to the early 1980s but that 1985 witnessed a spectacular rebirth of the stock market.

Let's look now at the total profits of U.S. corporations as reported quarterly by the Department of Commerce. Like the GNP numbers in the previous chapter, these are always reported in terms of an annual rate. Figure 19 shows profits before taxes as a solid line and profits after taxes as a dotted line. The reason for looking at the two together is that we get a clear picture of the substantial tax burden carried by corporations and, therefore, by shareholders. Profits after taxes are about 35 percent less than profits before taxes. In other words, Uncle Sam owns a 35 percent share in corporate America. These are current dollar figures with no allowance yet for the effects of inflation. Does $140 billion, the total profit of U.S. corporations in 1985, sound like a lot of money? Of course it is, but keep in mind that this is in the context of a current-dollar GNP of about $4000 billion in 1985. In other words, shareholders got only about 3.5 percent of the GNP pie. Notice that 1979 represented a peak for corporate profits that by the end of 1985 had not yet been regained. This is largely an illusion due to the distortions wrought by inflation, as we shall soon see.

What ultimately matters to shareholders is the purchasing power of their profits, what those profits will buy at the supermarket, the gas station, and the department store. We need to express profits in "constant dollars" as we have stock prices and GNP in earlier chapters. An increase in terms of constant dollars represents a *real* increase in purchasing power, not just a nominal increase due to inflation. When we express U.S. corporate profits after tax

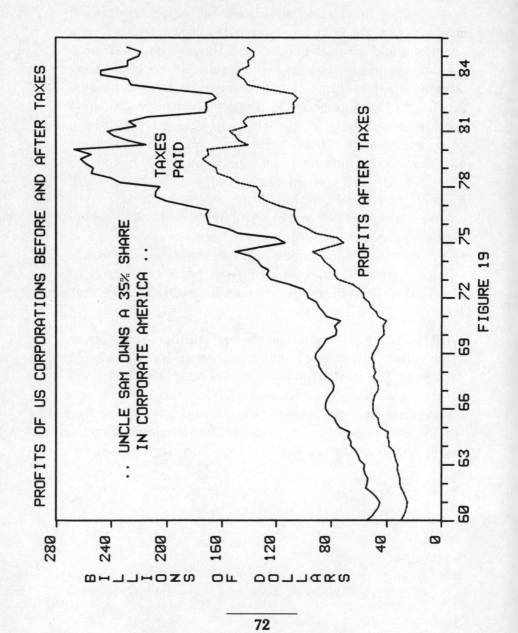

PROFITS OF US CORPORATIONS BEFORE AND AFTER TAXES

.. UNCLE SAM OWNS A 35% SHARE
IN CORPORATE AMERICA ..

TAXES PAID

PROFITS AFTER TAXES

FIGURE 19

BILLIONS OF DOLLARS

280
240
200
160
120
80
40
0

60 63 66 69 72 75 78 81 84

in constant 1982 dollars we get the picture seen in Figure 20. Notice that profits in constant dollars were roughly the same in 1985 as they had been 20 years earlier in 1965. No growth in *real* profits for 20 years! Hardly a rewarding period for shareholders. But wait—the strong surge in profits in the late 1970s that you see in Figure 20 was largely an illusion. Why? Because of the way inflation distorted the measurement of profit during those years. On the bright side, 1984 and 1985 witnessed a recovery in the profitability of U.S. corporations that is invisible in Figure 20!

If real profits can be illusory, how do we get a handle on *really real* profits? We need to remove the distortion that inflation creates in the accounting of business expenses. The basic problem is that accountants generally measure the cost of an item by what the company paid for it. Now if prices are stable, that is a perfectly reasonable thing to do. But suppose that prices of almost everything are rising at something like a 15 percent annual rate, as they were in 1979. Then the true cost of materials and plant and equipment is not what the company paid for them at some point in the past, but rather what it costs now to replace them. The difference between historical cost used by accountants and replacement cost creates a bookkeeping profit, but not a gain to the shareholders. These illusory inflation profits not only distort the reported accounting profits of the company, but they result in a higher tax bill for the company. Those illusory inflation profits are taxed by the IRS just as if they were actual profits that represented a gain to shareholders.

A simple example may help to clarify how inflation creates phony profit. Imagine that we are running a steel warehouse. We buy steel in various forms and sell it to users like construction firms that don't want to have to hold an inventory of each kind of material that they use. A particular piece of steel might sit in our

73

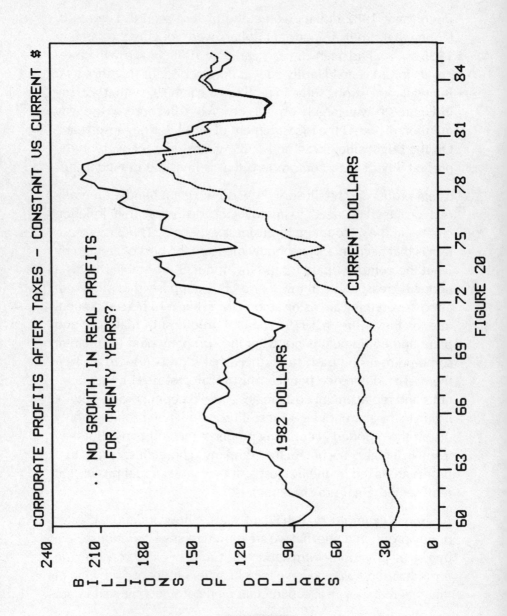

CORPORATE PROFITS AFTER TAXES - CONSTANT US CURRENT $

.. NO GROWTH IN REAL PROFITS FOR TWENTY YEARS?

1982 DOLLARS

CURRENT DOLLARS

FIGURE 20

warehouse for months before it is bought. If we paid $100 for that item and sold it for $120, then our accountant records a profit on the sale of $20. That is fine if we can turn around and replace that item for $100 as before. But if inflation is raging at a rate of 15 percent per year we will probably find that replacing this item costs more, say $110. How far ahead are we on this deal, really? Clearly we are ahead by only $10. Not only are our books distorted by $10, but we will pay income tax on that extra $10 of phony profit. What really happened was that while that piece of steel sat in our warehouse, the cost of steel and everything else rose by 10 percent. This is not a real gain to anyone because everything costs more. To put it another way, we bought the steel with 100-cent dollars and sold it for 90-cent dollars.

Because conventional accounting failed to recognize the inflation-caused discrepancy between the historical cost of materials and their replacement cost, the published profits of individual companies and the official indicators of corporate profits as a whole were seriously overstated during the inflation of the late 1970s and early 1980s. To get a more accurate measure of profit, the Department of Commerce subtracts from the accountants' numbers an estimate of inflation-caused inventory profit called the *inventory valuation adjustment*. In 1979, the IVA amounted to $43 billion, or about 25 percent of total after-tax profits. Before we look at what this does to the record of profitability we need to make one more adjustment because of the way accountants—and the IRS—calculate depreciation costs.

When we built our steel warehouse, we recognized that the cost of construction was not an expense, at least not yet. After all, the warehouse was probably worth as much as it cost to build. It was an asset. Construction cost becomes an expense only as time and the use of the warehouse cause it to deteriorate and therefore

---

75

depreciate in value. Recognizing this, our accountant charges a fraction of the construction cost of the warehouse against the income of the company as depreciation expense. But this is based on the historical cost of the warehouse, not what it would cost to replace today. If there were no inflation and costs were stable, then this would be fine. But if inflation is driving costs up, then depreciation expense based on historical cost is an underestimate of what using the warehouse is really costing. When it comes time to replace it, the construction costs will be much greater than what we have allowed over the years. If our warehouse cost $1 million, and inflation is running at 10 percent per year, then 10 years later it will cost $2.6 million to replace. Again, inflation has caused us to overstate our actual profits. This not only makes our profit look higher than it really was, it also obliges us to pay more income tax. The additional accounting profit caused by inflation was purely illusory, but the tax paid on it was very real indeed!

The Department of Commerce has developed a second adjustment to profits that is called the *capital consumption adjustment* to try to remove the discrepancy between historical cost and replacement cost of plant and equipment. In 1979 this amounted to almost $15 billion or 9 percent of total after-tax profits.

When U.S. corporate profits are adjusted for both of these factors, the result is the best indicator we have of true profitability, and it has the long-winded name of Corporate Profits After Tax With IVA And CCA In Constant Dollars. These are *really* real profits. It is too bad that individual companies are not required to report profits to shareholders in these terms because it would give their shareholders a more realistic indication of the return on their invested capital. Better yet, taxation of corporate income should also be based on this type of measure in order that only true profits be taxed. The resulting picture of the profitability of U.S. corporations that this indicator gives us is seen in Figure 21. Notice that the growth in real profits that we thought we had seen in the 1970s has vanished. The 1979 peak is now no higher than the mid-1960s peak. That is the bad news. The good news is that profits in 1984 and 1985 are now seen to be sharply higher than in 1979, and have moved ahead onto significantly higher ground. Little wonder that the stock market stagnated during the 1970s and was finally able to recover lost ground in the 1980s.

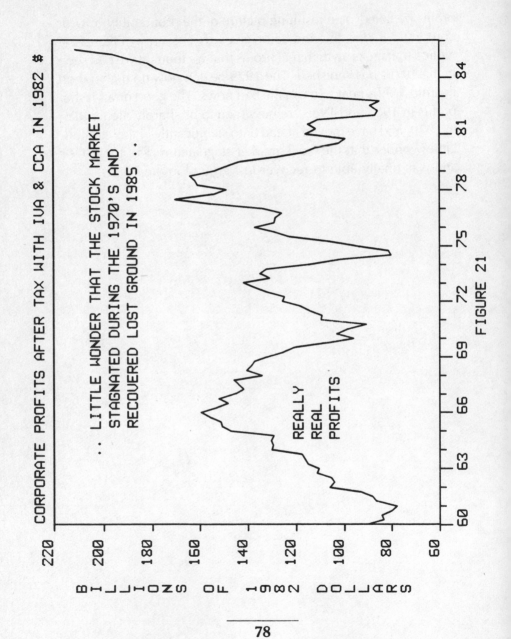

CORPORATE PROFITS AFTER TAX WITH IVA & CCA IN 1982 $

.. LITTLE WONDER THAT THE STOCK MARKET STAGNATED DURING THE 1970'S AND RECOVERED LOST GROUND IN 1985 ..

REALLY REAL PROFITS

BILLIONS OF 1982 DOLLARS

220 200 180 160 140 120 100 80 60

60 63 66 69 72 75 78 81 84

FIGURE 21

Profits, Real Profits, and Really Real Profits

Let's now link up the profit performance of U.S. corporations to the performance of the real economy. To measure the health of the real economy we will use the Rate of Capacity Utilization in manufacturing, introduced in the previous chapter. When we chart this together with really real profits we get the picture shown in Figure 22. It is immediately apparent that profits are very sensitive to the ups and downs of the real economy. Declining utilization of plant and equipment means sharply declining profits, and rising utilization pushes profits up rapidly. For example, from the peak of 1979 to the bottom of the 1981−1982 recession, capacity utilization fell about 20 percent but profits plummeted about 40 percent.

Looking over the longer term we see that profits went nowhere in an environment of slow growth in the real economy. While capacity utilization trended downward from the mid-1960s on, the profits of U.S. corporations stagnated. But what about that spectacular recovery in profits in 1984 and 1985? It seems to have happened without a strong recovery in capacity utilization. Here we see the fruits of the *disinflation* of the 1980s and the impact of direct tax relief. Disinflation allowed interest rates to drop sharply, reducing borrowing costs. The disarray of OPEC was part of the disinflation process and resulted in a general retreat in energy costs. Disinflation also eliminated the distortions of inflation on profits through inventories and depreciation. What we see here is a sharp rise in the *quality* of reported profits as they started to more accurately reflect real results. Corporations also benefited from the Economic Recovery Act of 1981, which allowed accelerated depreciation of plant and equipment, largely to compensate for the underestimation of depreciation due to inflation.

The fundamental linkage between the real economy and profits

79

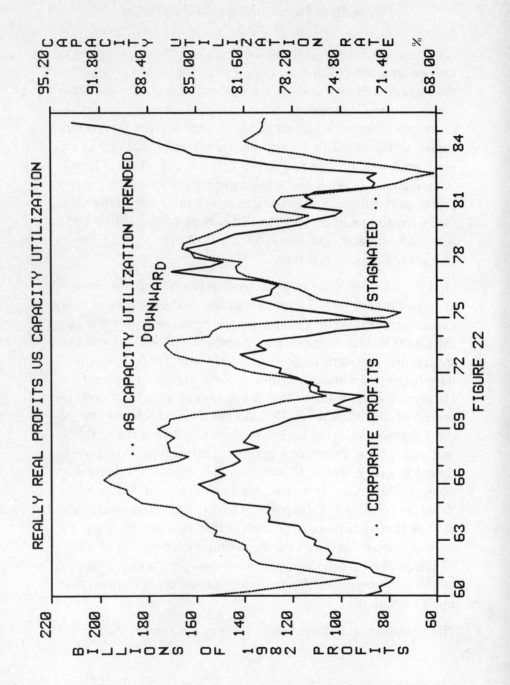

REALLY REAL PROFITS VS CAPACITY UTILIZATION

FIGURE 22

remains intact, though, and continued growth in profits through the 1980s will depend on whether we have a growing economy or a stagnating one. Based on my optimism about growth in the real economy, I feel that the prospects for continued growth in profits are better than they have been since the early 1960s.

The Bottom Line

Corporate profits are very sensitive to the health of the real economy. Inflation causes accounting profits to overstate true profits, and the properly adjusted indicator shows that there was no growth in really real profits after the mid-1960s until 1984. Hardly a coincidence that the stock market did about the same.

8

What Is the Future of American Business Worth?

Now let's put the final pieces of this puzzle together and see how *really real* corporate profits impact the stock market. Remember that profit is what is left over for the shareholders after the company has paid its expenses and made allowance for depreciation of its plant and equipment. Some of this profit is paid out to the shareholders in the form of a cash dividend, and the rest of it is reinvested in the business where it helps to pay for new machinery, buildings, product development, and so forth. If these investments enhance the efficiency of the enterprise and the demand for its products, then the shareholders will benefit from a larger flow of *future profits*. Greater future profits mean greater *future dividends* for the shareholders.

Which would you rather own, shares in a company that has little prospect for growth in the future or shares in one that shows promise of rapid profit growth? Of course we all would prefer to participate in a growing stream of profits and dividends, and this is reflected in the premium price that shares of fast growing companies command on the stock market. What is true for individual stocks is true for the stock market: When prospects for growth are rosy, the stock market flies high; when skies are gray, the stock market is down in the dumps.

As we have seen, the 1970s were not kind to the U.S. economy or to corporate profits. This came as a great disappointment after the halcyon 1950s and 1960s when economic growth was strong and steady and so was the growth of profits. We were masters of our destiny in those days, the undisputed leader in the world both economically and politically. The other industrial nations sought our technology and our management methods. We established the *Pax Americana* under which world trade boomed. We invented the high-speed computer and we put men on the moon.

But the late 1960s and 1970s held in store some unsettling surprises. First was our inability to control the situation in Vietnam and bring it to an acceptable conclusion. Profound disillusionment with government, American institutions, and the private enterprise system was part of the domestic fallout from that tragedy. At times it seemed that the very fabric of American society was in danger of tearing. American business became a focus of these tensions, and it became fashionable to question anything and everything that business was doing. Environmental impact, product safety, and pricing policies all came under closer scrutiny in Congress and in the courts. What was good for General Motors was no longer thought to be good for the country. Some people even seemed to take the attitude that what was *bad* for General Motors must be good for the country. The social attitude toward American business became ambivalent to a degree not seen since the 1930s. Who could have confidence in the future of American business at a time like that?

Then came the oil embargo, the cold, dark winter of 1973 – 1974, and OPEC. Suddenly, a bunch of Arab sheiks were holding the U.S. economy for ransom. We no longer seemed in control of our own destiny. What had our position in the world come to if a bunch of small countries with no industrial or military might could push us around? What confidence could we have in our future? Energy costs soared, the economy plunged into the worst recession of the postwar era, and corporate profits nose-dived. At this point, investors made a severe reappraisal of the prospects for the future. The stock market went into a dizzying plunge that wiped out nearly half of its market value. In the midst of this debacle, the President was forced into a humiliating resignation. The optimism about the future that had sustained the bull market for a quarter of a century gave way to pervasive pessimism. We have yet to regain that confidence about our future.

Let's take a look now at the interaction of the stock market and real profits over the past 25 years as depicted in Figure 23. The solid line tracks the real value of stocks since 1960, and the dotted line shows what has happened to really real corporate profits over the same period. We are measuring the real value of the stock market the same way here that we did in Chapter 5, using the Standard & Poor's 500 Stock Index and adjusting it by the Consumer Price Index to reflect inflation. Recall that this shows the purchasing power of a representative stock portfolio and that it peaked in the late 1960s at a value of about $1. Really real profits are the measure we developed in Chapter 7, where we found that profits need a double adjustment to remove all of the distortions caused by inflation.

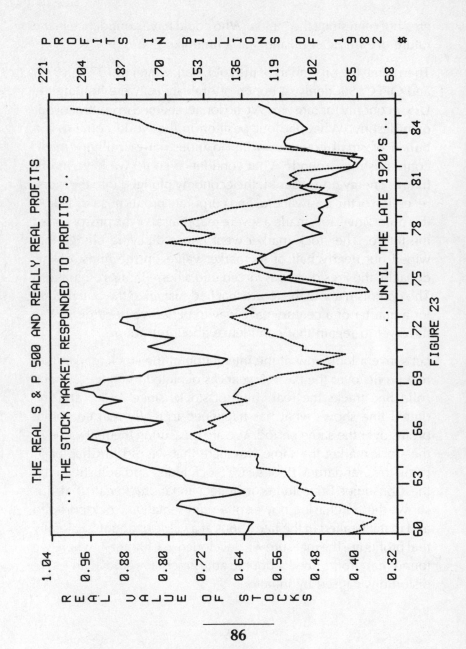

THE REAL S & P 500 AND REALLY REAL PROFITS

.. THE STOCK MARKET RESPONDED TO PROFITS ..

.. UNTIL THE LATE 1970'S ..

FIGURE 23

What Is the Future of American Business Worth?

We see right away that the stock market pays attention to profits. Each major move in profits is accompanied by a major move in the stock market. Notice, though, that 1974 represents a watershed in the responsiveness of the market to profits. Prior to 1974, the market seemed to move almost proportionally with profits. But after 1974, the market shows a clear reluctance to follow along when profits improve. Following the 1973—1975 recession, profits staged something of a comeback, finally regaining the heights of the mid-1960s by the end of the 1970s. But the stock market failed to follow suit. After bouncing back from the crisis lows of 1974, the market started to run out of steam and spent the last three years of the decade drifting lower. When profits broke again in the face of the double recession of 1980 and 1981—1982, the stock market had no trouble talking itself into another retreat. By the summer of 1982, the purchasing power of a stock portfolio had fallen by about 60 percent from its 1968 peak. A leading business magazine brazenly proclaimed "The Death of Stocks." This may have been one of the worst business prognostications on record, but it accurately reflected the depth of the gloom surrounding the market.

Profits rebounded spectacularly from the 1982 recession lows, but the stock market responded halfheartedly. Yes, the rally that ignited in the late summer of 1982 and carried on into 1983 was a steep one, but it petered out in 1984 in spite of soaring corporate profits. It wasn't until 1985 that the stock market began to move ahead again in a convincing manner. Why did it take so long? Why did the market respond so skeptically to the improvement in profits when it did occur? Why did stocks still sell at a discount of about 40 percent relative to their real value 20 years earlier?

I am convinced that the primary answer to these questions lies in the *disappointed expectations* of those two decades. It was not that profits declined during those years, but that they failed to grow at the rates that the stock market bulls of the 1960s had expected. That steep rise in really real profits that you see in Figure 23 from 1960 to 1966 represented a heady growth rate of about 13 percent per year compounded. How many investors, professional or otherwise, were really ready for a world in which profit growth would effectively stop? From the peak in the middle of the 1960s to the next peak in the late 1970s profits were to grow (if we can even use that term) at a paltry average of about 0.5 percent per year! Sure, it was great (and a great relief!) to see profits surge ahead in the mid-1980s, but the average growth rate from the mid-1960s peak to the very robust level of 1984 was still only about 1 percent per year.

By this point, investors needed more than a couple of years of rising profits to convince them that happy times were here again. When people now looked ahead into the 1990s they did so with a somewhat jaundiced eye. The world was just not as safe a place for us as it had appeared in 1966. We had been battered by two oil shocks that we seemed unable to do anything about. Could it happen again? When would inflation again disrupt the economy? How could the rising deficit of the federal government ever be brought under control? Would America's industrial decline be arrested, much less reversed?

Instead of showing the world how to innovate and manage, we were now the ones adopting foreign techniques. Who would have believed in 1966 that General Motors would be asking Toyota to help it design a new car *and* the plant it would be built in? For that matter, who had even heard of Toyota in 1966? The Japanese are just copycats, remember? *Business Week* recently attributed the great success of Ford's new Taurus/Sable line of cars to their adoption of Japanese techniques in project management, engineering, and production. One of the key steps in the development of these cars was "reverse engineering" in which leading imports were torn down piece by piece to see how they had been designed and made. By adopting the best features of their competitors from Germany and Japan, Ford was able to leapfrog to the cutting edge of the industry. Sounds familiar, doesn't it?

America has had some big disappointments to digest during the last two decades and so has the stock market. But I think that the biggest mistake that we investors could make would be to focus on the reverses of the recent past and ignore the very real promise of the future. We live in an enormously resilient society, and it still possesses the strongest economy in the world. Most important, we have the capacity to learn and to change. The challenges that the 1970s threw at us have elicited change for the better. The oil price shocks have resulted in reduced dependence on foreign energy sources and a level of energy efficiency that was unthinkable only a decade ago. The challenge of foreign industrial competition has reawakened the spirit of innovation and renewed the quest for efficiency in the country where mass production was invented. Double-digit inflation has given way to a more realistic monetary policy at the Federal Reserve, one that recognizes the importance of monetary stability. Public pressure for a more rational tax system that encourages savings and investment has been building steadily in the 1980s. Deregulation in many areas of the economy has spurred efficiency and freed business to meet the challenges of the marketplace instead of the requirements of a bureaucracy. Research and development is again at the forefront of business priorities, and engineering schools are deluged with top-quality applicants who enjoy the prospect of being in strong demand at graduation. And, yes, General Motors is scrambling to get back out in front. It is only in the last few years that we created the personal computer revolution and invented genetic engineering. This is no time to sell America short!

If the case for optimism is justified, then the stock market offered remarkable investment value at 1985 levels. Take a look at Figure 24. This is a chart of the "P/E ratio" of the Standard & Poor's 500 Stock Index. P/E ratio is investment jargonese for "price to earnings ratio" or simply the price of a share of stock divided by the earnings (profits) per share. The P/E ratio for an index like the S&P 500 is a weighted average of the P/E's of the stocks that make up the index. Alternatively, you can think of it as the P/E for a portfolio of shares, obtained by adding up the value of the shares and dividing by all the company profits attributable to those shares. A P/E ratio represents a *real* indicator of the stock market because inflation in the numerator (price) cancels inflation in the denominator (earnings). However, these are accountant's profits, so phony gains in inventories and depreciation caused by inflation are present in the earnings.

Notice that the watershed of 1973–1974 shows up very clearly in the P/E ratio. It averaged about 18 through the optimistic 1960s, then plunged precipitously to 8 in 1974, and thereafter fluctuated around a new average of about 10. This distinct revaluation of earnings was enough to knock about 45 percent off the value of stocks without any actual change in earnings! Why such a high value for earnings in the pre-1973 era and so much lower a value afterward? The market had lost confidence in the ability of the U.S. economy to generate growth in corporate profits.

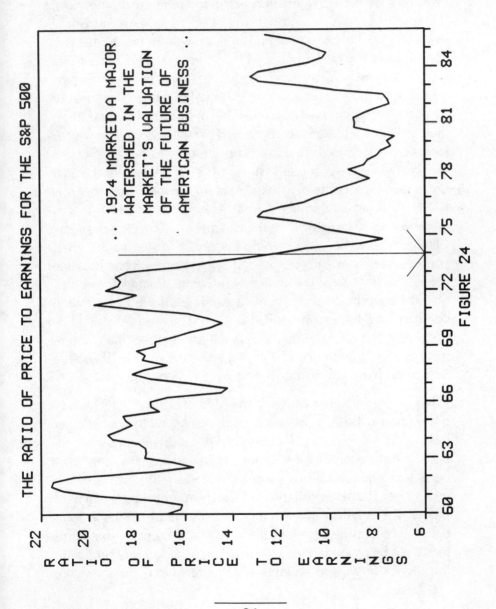

THE RATIO OF PRICE TO EARNINGS FOR THE S&P 500

... 1974 MARKED A MAJOR
WATERSHED IN THE
MARKET'S VALUATION
OF THE FUTURE OF
AMERICAN BUSINESS ...

RATIO OF PRICE TO EARNINGS

FIGURE 24

Perhaps a bit more explanation about the relationship between P/E ratios and earnings growth might be useful. An individual stock that has little prospect for future growth (in real terms) will often have a P/E ratio of about 10 on average. This means that investors are willing to pay a price for the shares equal to the next 10 years' earnings. For example, if annual earnings per share are $1 and are expected to be fairly stable at that level in the future, then the stock will trade at about $10 per share. Another way to look at it is to turn the P/E ratio upside down and say that the *earnings yield* is 10 percent, since $1 is 10 percent of the $10 price. Now if a company that shows no prospect for growth is worth 10 times its earnings, what is a company worth that is perceived to be growing in real terms at, say, 5 percent per year? Certainly more, because owning a share in this company gives you a piece of a growing pie instead of a static pie. A bit of college algebra suffices to show that this growing stream of earnings would be worth 20 times current earnings. If the fast-growing company also has earnings of $1 per share this year, then investors would be willing to pay $20 per share. Notice that a seemingly modest growth rate of 5 percent per year doubles the value of the company compared to one which is not growing.

What we see in Figure 24 is just this kind of dramatic difference, but applied to the stock market as a whole. A growth stock market before 1973 commanded a growth P/E ratio, reflecting anticipated growth of around 4 to 5 percent in real terms. When prospects for continued growth were dimmed by the events of the mid-1970s, P/E ratios collapsed to a level appropriate to stagnant profits. The very low point in the market's P/E in 1979–1980 to below 8 reflects in large part the market's perception that earnings were being overstated by inflation-caused phony profits on inventories and understatement of depreciation. But even the high quality profits of 1984—1985 were priced at a very modest P/E of 10 to 12.

The potential gain to investors from the low P/E's of the mid-1980s is clearly enormous. If the promise of a new era of economic growth is fulfilled in the next decade, we can reasonably expect not only growth in corporate profits but also a growing valuation of those earnings in the form of a rising P/E ratio. The double-whammy effect would propel the stock market ahead at a dizzying pace. Suppose, for illustration, that earnings were to grow at a 5 percent rate in real terms for the next decade. If the average P/E in the market remained constant, the market would gain 60 percent in real purchasing power by the end of the period. If, in addition, this renewed growth fostered expectations of future growth comparable to the pre-1973 era, then we could expect the average P/E ratio in the market to move back up to the 18 level. This adds another 50 percent to market value! Preposterous, you say? Not at all. What we are really talking about here is undoing the damage of the past 20 years, and who is to say it can't be done?

The Bottom Line

The stock market values not just corporate profits but equally importantly the growth in profits. The collapse in the stock market in the 1970s reflected the perception that an era of growth for the U.S. economy had ended. A new era of renewed growth holds out the prospect of a spectacular upward revaluation of the stock market in the years ahead.

9

Indicators that Forecast the Real Economy

Around the first of each month the U.S. Department of Commerce releases the Index of Leading Indicators, an event that receives a great deal of attention in the media. The reason for all the publicity is that this index is supposed to be able to forecast the direction of the real economy several months ahead. The Index of Leading Indicators is actually a composite of 12 separate indicators that have been found in the past to change direction before the economy does. Any indicator that anticipates movements in the economy is called a *leading indicator*. By combining these into an index, government economists hope to create one indicator that forecasts the real economy with greatest possible reliability. On average, the Index grows at about the same rate as the real economy, a bit over 3 percent per annum or 0.25 percent per month. When the Index grows faster than that, it is signaling unusually rapid growth ahead for the real economy. If the growth rate shown by the Index falls below this rate, then it is telling us to expect a sluggish economy. An actual decline in the Index is a warning of recession if it persists for more than a few months.

Most of the components of the Index of Leading Indicators are just the sort of indicators you would think would lead the economy: items such as contracts and orders for plant and equipment, permits issued for new housing, formation of new businesses, and manufacturers' new orders. Since contracts, orders, and permits must precede actual construction, these seem like pretty good bets. The formation of new businesses is a barometer of optimism about the future and the willingness of businesspeople to invest and spend.

Another component of the Index is weekly hours of production workers. Firms will assign overtime hours before undertaking the costs of adding new employees, so hours should change ahead of major moves in the economy. The change in manufacturing and trade inventories is included because a build-up of inventories tends to lead to cutbacks in production, and lean inventories suggest a speedup of production is forthcoming. Sensitive materials prices will reflect stronger or weaker demand before other prices, and therefore the change in a group of such prices is included in the leading index. A build-up of business and consumer credit has often preceded a slowdown in the economy because buyers have stretched their capacity to borrow. Similarly, contraction of credit has signaled that the consumer is liquid again and ready to resume buying.

The number of unemployment claims filed with state unemployment offices has been found to lead peaks in the economy. An advantage of this indicator is that it is announced weekly, and some business economists watch it closely because it is so timely. Evidently, state unemployment claims work as a leading indicator because jobs become hard to find before actual production turns down. The number of companies reporting slower deliveries from vendors is another component of the leading index. During an expansion of the real economy, delivery times get longer as firms struggle to keep production ahead of orders without depleting their inventories. When deliveries become more prompt it is a signal that the expansion is slowing down. The remaining 2 of the 12 components of the Index of Leading Indicators are the money supply measured by M2 (adjusted for inflation) and stock prices. We will be taking a closer look at these two later.

Is the Index of Leading Indicators all that it's cracked up to be? Does it really give us advance warning of changes in the direction of the real economy? Figure 25 charts the Index of Leading Indicators (solid line) along with the Index of Industrial Production (dotted line) and it is readily apparent that peaks in the former precede peaks in the latter by several months. Similarly, the Index of Leading Indicators has typically turned up several months before production has bottomed out at the low point of a recession. Notice, for example, that the Index of Leading Indicators weakened in 1984, remaining essentially flat for the year. While this did not signal an outright recession for 1985, it did give warning of very sluggish growth. Many professional forecasters seemed to be caught up in the presidential election hoopla in the fall of 1984 and predicted strong economic expansion in 1985. They were wrong and the Index of Leading Indicators was right—1985 turned out to be a year of very lackluster growth in the real economy, as you can see in Figure 25.

There are some practical drawbacks in the way the Index of Leading Indicators is produced that make its performance in real time somewhat less impressive than it appears in retrospect. For

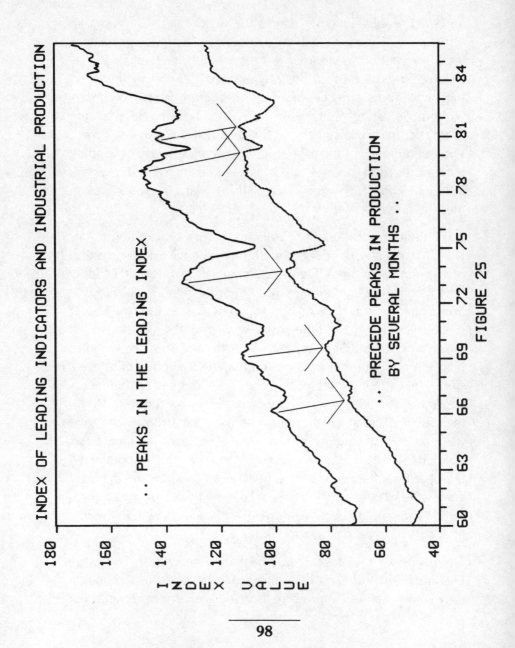

INDEX OF LEADING INDICATORS AND INDUSTRIAL PRODUCTION

.. PEAKS IN THE LEADING INDEX

.. PRECEDE PEAKS IN PRODUCTION
    BY SEVERAL MONTHS ..

FIGURE 25

180

160

140

120

100

80

60

40

INDEX VALUE

60 63 66 69 72 75 78 81 84

example, when the Index is announced, the number is not for the month just past but for the prior month. The announcement of the Index on July 1 would not be for June but rather for May. We have already lost two months' lead time when the number is announced. In spite of the wait, the Index is not even complete. Generally, it has been estimated without two of the components being available. Other components are available on a preliminary basis and are subject to revision, sometimes considerable revision. As a result, the number which is first announced, two months after the fact, may be revised considerably over the course of the coming months.

A change in the economy that is fully apparent in retrospect when we look at the revised data may not have been so apparent when it was happening. In fact, it sometimes turns out that the preliminary estimate gave a downright misleading signal. January 1984 is a case in point. When the Index for that month was announced at the end of February, it showed a spectacular 1.1 percent rise for the month. This is more than four times the trend rate of growth for the Index, so it seemed to suggest that 1984 might be a very good year for the U.S. economy. With each succeeding month, however, this January reading was revised downward until by the end of May it was estimated that the Index had risen by only 0.3 percent in January. These revisions of indicators for past months are rarely highlighted by the press, so they often pass unnoticed except by the professionals. If the original announcement for January 1984 had said that the Index rose by only 0.3 percent, then the modest pace of growth experienced in 1984 would have come as less of a surprise. By the end of May that information was just too late to do us much good.

One of the things we can do about the shortcomings of the the Index of Leading Indicators is to make use of individual leading indicators which are available on a more timely basis. The most useful of these, in my experience, has been the rate of growth in the real supply of money, specifically M2. Recall that money is the stuff we use to pay our bills. It consists of currency and checking account balances (which make up M1) plus money market mutual fund and interest bearing bank account balances, the grand total of which is called M2. Now money is used to settle transactions, and if there is, say, 10 percent inflation over the period of a year, then people will need 10 percent more money to carry out their business. If the money supply had risen by less than 10 percent over the same year, then consumers and businesses would be feeling squeezed for cash. On the other hand, if the supply of money had risen by more than 10 percent, then the actors in the economy would have more than enough money to do business in spite of higher prices for everything. The term that fits here is *liquidity*. In the first situation, people had become less liquid because their means of payment had not kept up the dollar volume of their activities. In the second situation, people had become more liquid because their ability to settle transactions had increased on balance.

When people feel illiquid, they will try to rebuild their money balances by slowing purchases and perhaps by selling assets. In contrast, when people feel more liquid they will tend to spend some of that liquidity to buy things that either are useful, perhaps a new car, or offer the prospect of gain, say, shares in a growth stock mutual fund. This suggests that liquidity would be a good leading indicator of economic activity. To measure liquidity, we divide M2 by the price index and track the resulting real supply of money. This is a real indicator like the others encountered in this book. When real M2 rises it means that M2 has risen faster than inflation and therefore the purchasing power of money balances has increased. When real M2 declines it means that the purchasing power of money balances has fallen. An increase in the purchasing power of money balances is an increase in the liquidity of the economy, and a decrease in the purchasing power of money balances is a decrease in liquidity.

Let's see now how this principle works out in practice. In Figure 26 I have charted the real quantity of M2 (measured in 1982 dollars) as the solid line and the Index of Industrial Production as the dotted line. Notice how major swings in liquidity have preceded major moves in the real economy. Before discussing these I think it is important to note that the relatively steady growth of liquidity in the 1960s went hand-in-hand with steady growth in the real economy and, as you will recall, low inflation. A growing real economy needs growth in liquidity sufficient to lubricate a growing volume of commerce. But in 1969, liquidity started on a roller coaster ride which has produced successively more severe cycles of inflation, followed by recession, followed by even higher inflation.

The first big contraction in liquidity occurred in 1969 when the Fed became concerned about an upward trend in inflation and tried to put on the brakes. A major recession followed in 1970 along with a cooling of inflation (see Figure 5 for the inflation picture). Having scared itself by producing the first recession in a decade, the Fed then launched a three-year expansion of liquidity that substantially outstripped the growth rate of the 1960s. Again, about a year later the real economy responded with rapid, and inflationary, growth that kept up for a year after liquidity quit expanding. During 1973 and 1974 the monetary brakes were on hard, with liquidity contracting more sharply than in 1969. The Fed was worried by escalating inflation (again, you may want to

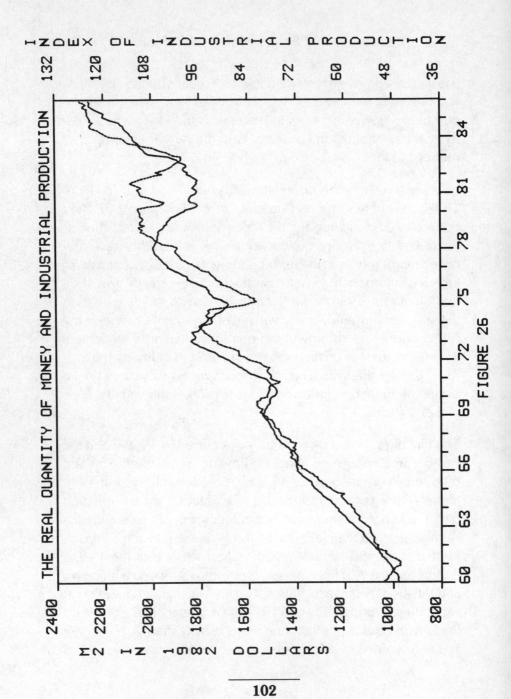

THE REAL QUANTITY OF MONEY AND INDUSTRIAL PRODUCTION

FIGURE 26

peek at Figure 5) and a tumbling dollar on foreign exchange markets. The result of this sharper contraction of liquidity was an even sharper recession in 1974 and 1975. Although it had some help from OPEC, the Fed had engineered the worst recession since World War II. So what did it do for an encore? It launched another rapid acceleration of liquidity that got the real economy growing again, but was the driving force behind the even higher inflation rates of the late 1970s. Although liquidity stopped growing at the beginning of 1978, the real economy kept moving ahead for another year. Again, we see liquidity leading the real economy by about a year. What is somewhat surprising is that the real economy resisted a major slump as long as it did. Although liquidity had contracted during 1979 and 1980, the big slide in production was delayed until 1982. I think the primary reason for this was that by 1980 most people were so caught up in the psychology of buying to beat inflation that it took them an extra year to realize that the game had changed. Suddenly the new game was to batten down the hatches and conserve enough liquidity to survive the most severe recession since the Great Depression. Then renewed growth in liquidity in 1982, which continued into 1983, signaled the coming recovery of 1983 and 1984.

Another way to see how changes in liquidity lead changes in the real economy is in terms of growth rates. These are charted in Figure 27 as the percentage change from the same month of the prior year. Again, real money is the solid line and industrial production the dotted line. The minirecession of 1967 shows up more clearly here than in Figure 26 and as usual it was preceded by a contraction in liquidity the previous year. The minirecession of 1967 just missed being severe enough to be declared a full-fledged recession by the official record keepers at the National

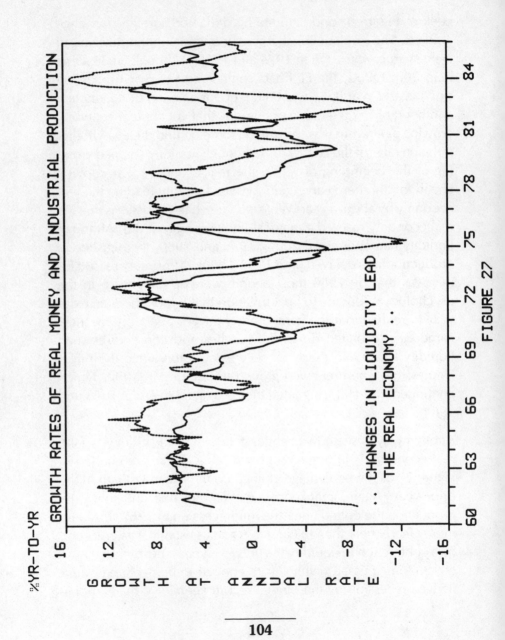

%YR-TO-YR

GROWTH RATES OF REAL MONEY AND INDUSTRIAL PRODUCTION

.. CHANGES IN LIQUIDITY LEAD
THE REAL ECONOMY ..

FIGURE 27

Bureau of Economic Research, but it was a shot heard 'round the world. Up until that point, the Keynesians were the dominant school of thought on the subject of what caused recessions and depressions. According to them, government spending made the economic world go 'round, and money didn't matter. Moneta-rists had been on the defensive since the 1930s, as it had been thought that the Great Depression could not be explained by monetary factors. Reexamination of the role of the collapse of the banking system in aggravating the depression in a landmark study by Milton Friedman and Anna Schwartz had started to rehabili-tate the monetarist viewpoint by the mid-1960s. When liquidity contracted in 1966, leading monetarists predicted a contraction in the economy for 1967. Keynesians, on the other hand, looked at the strong growth in federal spending driven by the Vietnam War build-up and President Johnson's Great Society programs, and they concluded that the economy would remain strong in 1967. The fact that the monetarists proved right and the Key-nesians proved wrong about 1967 sent a shock wave through the economics profession which is still reverberating. After that date it simply was no longer acceptable to maintain that money didn't matter.

The power of money to move the economy is evident in Figure 27. Each major rise in the growth of liquidity is followed by a corresponding rise in the growth of the real economy. Similarly, each major drop in the growth rate of liquidity is followed by a decline in the growth rate of production. One year seems to be a good rule of thumb for the lead time, but sometimes it is a bit longer. The fact that real M2 grew in 1984 and 1985 at a rate comparable to the 1960s and did not show signs of rapid acceler-ation or deceleration suggested that the following year or two would be ones of continuing real growth in the economy with little chance of accelerating inflation.

The remaining component of the Index of Leading Indicators that we haven't yet discussed is the one most readily available to all of us. It is announced daily and is never revised later. Unfortunately, it is what we would ultimately like to be able to predict! It is of course the stock market. The specific indicator used is the Standard & Poor's 500 Stock Index because of its great breadth. The Dow Jones Industrials consist of a mere 30 companies, albeit very large ones. The stock market is a powerful leading indicator of the real economy and has proven to be one of the most reliable of the components in the Index. Its track record is evident in Figure 28 where I have charted the change in the S&P 500 from the same month of the prior year (solid line) along with the corresponding change in the Index of Industrial Production (dotted line). Notice that major moves in the economy have almost invariably been preceded by major moves in the stock market. Also notice that the stock market seems to overdo things a bit. For example, it dropped sharply in early 1962, as if to signal a serious recession ahead. The growth rate of the economy did slacken somewhat, but nothing approaching a recession developed. Those of us born before 1950 remember President Kennedy's attack on the steel industry's right to set prices for its products. Executives were awakened by FBI agents in the middle of the night and called to account for their latest price increases. This was widely interpreted as the opening shot in a broader offensive on the autonomy of American business. Indeed it seems in retrospect to have set the stage for the expanded regulatory role of the federal government over the next decade and certainly set a precedent for peacetime price controls later expanded under Presidents Nixon and Carter. In any case, it spooked the stock market badly in 1962.

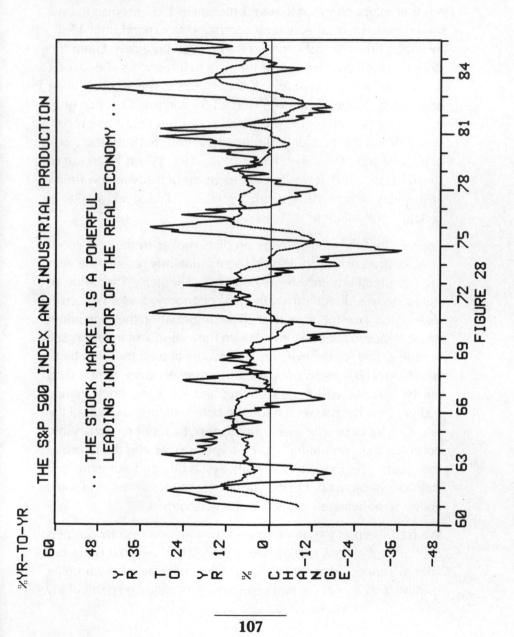

%YR-TO-YR

THE S&P 500 INDEX AND INDUSTRIAL PRODUCTION

... THE STOCK MARKET IS A POWERFUL
LEADING INDICATOR OF THE REAL ECONOMY ...

FIGURE 28

Another major retreat in the stock market in 1977 seemed to be a false signal. The real economy continued to expand until 1980, by which time the stock market had picked up again. Either the stock market's crystal ball was tuned in to three years ahead, or it jumped the gun prematurely. It is episodes of this sort that must have led to Nobel Prize winner Paul Samuelson's famous quip that the stock market had predicted seven of the last five recessions! When the economy did finally slump in 1980, the stock market seemed largely oblivious of the fact. When it ran out of steam in late 1980, it was too late to give much advance warning of the very severe 1981–1982 recession. The stock market is certainly not infallible.

The fact that the stock market predicts moves in the real economy, or at least tries to, should seem eminently reasonable after our investigations in the previous two chapters. The value of stocks derives directly from the real economy, and it behooves traders and investors to muster all the information they can about future trends in the economy. When the majority of investors see trouble ahead, or believe they see trouble ahead, they will try to sell shares and thereby drive the stock market down. Sunny skies on the horizon will trigger buying and send the stock market higher. Thus the market reflects the beliefs of investors about the future. A lot of people and institutions put a lot of resources into polishing their crystal balls to try to peer as far into the future as they can. The market is not always right, and sometimes it overdoes things a bit, but the efforts of investors do result in some ability to anticipate changes in the economy.

We have seen in earlier chapters how inflation distorts our perception of the stock market over a period of time, so it is reasonable to suppose that the *real* S&P 500 might be an even better leading indicator of the real economy. This might be particularly so during times like the late 1970s when inflation rates are high, and a rise in stock prices does not necessarily mean a rise in real stock prices. To see how much of a difference this makes, I have charted the change in the real S&P 500 as the solid line in Figure 29, along with the Index of Industrial Production as the dotted line. Notice that the signals given by the real stock market in Figure 29 do not differ substantially from what we saw in Figure 28 until the mid-1970s. The plunge in the real stock market in 1973–1974 shows up as an even more severe shock wave because we are seeing the change in real values in the stock market. Big trouble ahead for the real economy!

Correspondingly, the stock market recovery of 1975 when seen in real terms appears not quite so reassuring. Instead of the positive trend shown in Figure 28, the late 1970s were a period of continued erosion for the real stock market, anticipating the recession of 1980. The real S&P then gave a clear signal of short lived 1980–1981 recovery and then quickly reversed to warn of the 1981–1982 recession. Clearly the real value of stocks leads changes in the real economy, and it does so more reliably than stock prices without adjustment for the distortions of inflation. It is surprising, therefore, that the Department of Commerce does not adjust for inflation when it incorporates the S&P 500 in the Index of Leading Indicators. As of the end of 1985, the stock market saw continued real economic growth ahead in 1986, judging from the healthy rise shown in Figure 29. Evidently, investors felt that the war against inflation was coming to a successful conclusion.

William McChesney Martin, who was Chairman of the Board of Governors of the Federal Reserve from 1951 to 1970, said that it is the job of the Fed to take away the punch bowl when the party really gets going. It does this by reducing the liquidity of the

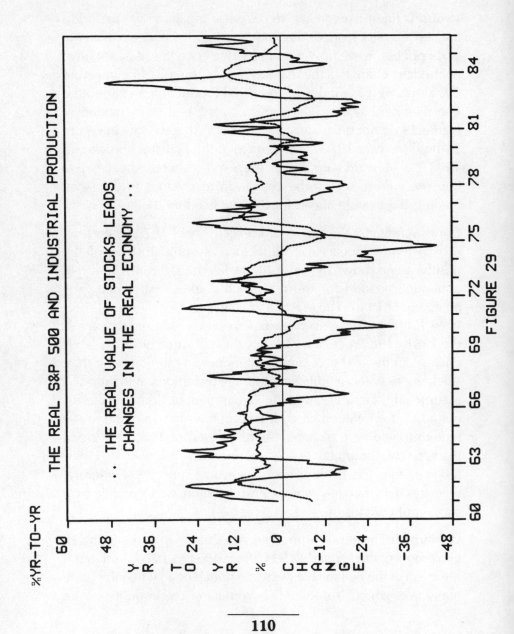

THE REAL S&P 500 AND INDUSTRIAL PRODUCTION

.. THE REAL VALUE OF STOCKS LEADS
CHANGES IN THE REAL ECONOMY ..

FIGURE 29

banking system, thereby pushing up interest rates. The sectors of the economy which are most sensitive to interest rates will be the first to feel the pinch, and one of the most interest-sensitive sectors of the economy is housing. Rising interest rates mean rising mortgage rates and mortgage payments are the biggest part of the cost of owning a home. This tells us that a decline in the rate of housing starts should give early warning of a general downturn in the real economy. Until the early 1980s, rising interest rates had another more direct impact on home buyers. Savings and loan institutions were the main source of mortgage funds, and they obtained these funds largely from their depositors. The rates which they could pay on deposits were subject to a strict ceiling imposed by regulation. When interest rates generally were rising, this ceiling rate on deposits became less and less attractive, so that the public tended to take their money out of the mortgage lending institutions and reinvest it in securities such as Treasury bills, which paid a going market rate. The result was a direct reduction in the availability of mortgage loans to prospective home buyers. When the Fed took away the punch bowl, home-building took a dive. With the deregulation of the savings and loan industry since 1980, mortgage lenders have more open access to money markets, and this direct effect is less important. Housing remains an important leading indicator, though, because mortgage interest is still a major portion of home ownership costs. Once a recession is underway, interest rates tend to fall partly because the Fed acts to keep the recession from getting worse. When the inflationary inebriation of the economy is perceived to have dissipated and the hangover has begun, the Fed brings back the punch bowl by increasing the liquidity of the banking system and reducing interest rates. We would expect housing to lead the economy out of a recession just as it leads the economy into it.

Two indicators of housing activity are announced monthly by the Department of Commerce: the number of housing units started and the number authorized by local permits. The latter is the one used in the Index of Leading Indicators, but the former is generally more widely available in the media. Both tell essentially the same story. Housing starts are announced about the middle of the month for the prior month and are expressed at an annual rate, adjusted for seasonal variation. For example, on January 17, 1986 the news media carried the announcement that housing starts were at a rate of 1.84 million units in December. This was pretty good news since 1.84 million is above average for the past 25 years, as you can see in Figure 30 where housing starts are charted as a solid line. Past experience suggests that a solid level of housing starts augurs well for the year ahead. Notice that the major dips in the Index of Industrial Production were preceded by slumps in housing; that is when the Fed took away the punch bowl. Each recession was signaled at least several months in advance by a plunge in housing starts. Likewise, every recovery from recession was anticipated by recovery in housing starts. As the recession caused interest rates to fall and the Fed to ease up on curbing the money supply, housing started to revive before the general economy. A good rule of thumb seems to be that a rate of starts above 1.5 million can be taken as reassurance of a healthy real economy in the year ahead, but when the rate falls below 1.5 million, watch out. Conversely, if the economy has been in recession, then a recovery in housing starts to above the 1.5 million level signals recovery for the economy.

Some so-called leading indicators are highly overrated, in my view. One of them is the Initial Unemployment Claims indicator which is included in the Index of Leading Indicators. This is a favorite of business economists because it is very timely. It is one

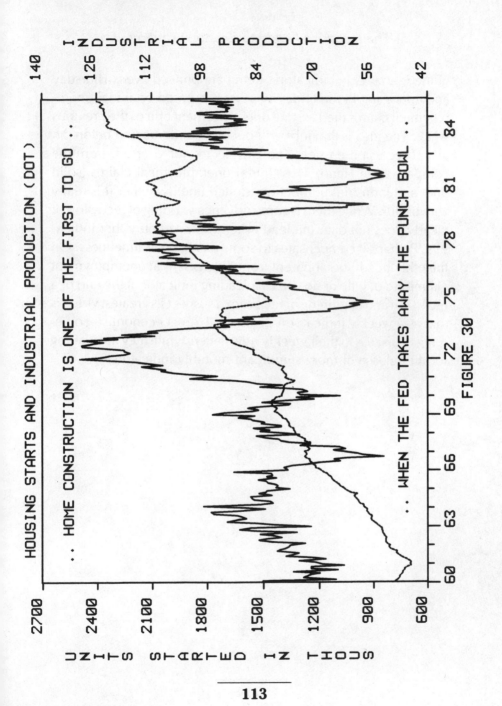

HOUSING STARTS AND INDUSTRIAL PRODUCTION (DOT)

.. HOME CONSTRUCTION IS ONE OF THE FIRST TO GO ..

.. WHEN THE FED TAKES AWAY THE PUNCH BOWL ..

FIGURE 30

of the few weekly indicators, being announced every Thursday and appearing in the Friday papers. It is based on initial unemployment claims filed at state unemployment offices the previous week. The idea is that jobs will become harder to find before an actual recession ensues. You can decide for yourself, from the comparison in Figure 31 of initial unemployment claims (solid line) and industrial production (dotted line), whether it is really very useful. While there is some advance warning of recession, it clearly does not offer the lead time of some of our other indicators. Perhaps it compensates to some extent by its timeliness. On the other hand, it is apparent from Figure 31 that unemployment claims are of little or no use as a leading indicator of the end of a recession and beginning of recovery. I suspect its greatest virtue is that as a weekly indicator it gives Wall Street economists something to discuss in their weekly newsletters while they are waiting for the release of more significant monthly indicators!

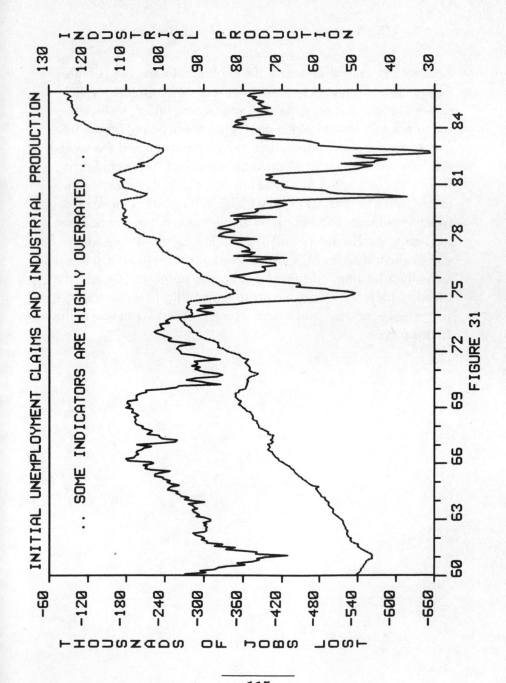

INITIAL UNEMPLOYMENT CLAIMS AND INDUSTRIAL PRODUCTION

... SOME INDICATORS ARE HIGHLY OVERRATED ...

FIGURE 31

Another indicator that is part of the official Index, but is highly overrated in my view, is Manufacturers' New Orders for Consumer Goods. In theory, the volume of new orders received by manufacturers should give a good clue about actual production in the months ahead. But orders can be canceled and the fact is that there is just not much lead in this so-called leading indicator. Figure 32 compares it as a solid line to Industrial Production as a dotted line. I find it hard to tell which is which—they move pretty much in tandem. This indicator isn't even a very timely one since it is announced about the end of the following month, a good two weeks after the Index of Industrial Production itself. That makes it virtually a lagging indicator for practical purposes. Clearly the "leading indicators" vary greatly in their ability to signal changes in the real economy, and manufacturers' orders is not one of the front runners.

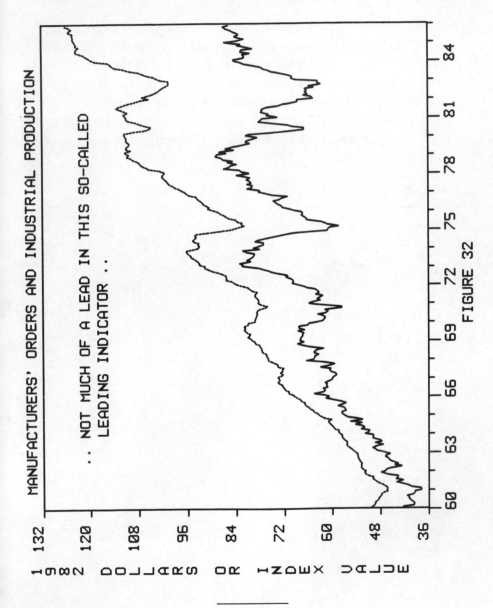

MANUFACTURERS' ORDERS AND INDUSTRIAL PRODUCTION

.. NOT MUCH OF A LEAD IN THIS SO-CALLED
LEADING INDICATOR ..

FIGURE 32

The Bottom Line

The government's Index of Leading Indicators often anticipates major moves in the real economy by several months, but late reporting reduces its value. You can get ahead of the game by watching some powerful individual leading indicators. The real quantity of money (M2 adjusted for inflation), the real value of the stock market (the S&P 500 adjusted for inflation), and housing starts have an excellent track record of signaling recession or recovery.

10

Indicators for Stock Market Timing

Forecasting the stock market may be the economics equivalent of alchemy—anyone who could do it with certainty would soon become infinitely rich. But unlike alchemy, it is the very fact that so many bright people are trying to do it that makes it so difficult. Individual investors, brokerage firm analysts, professional portfolio managers, and business economists by the thousands labor assiduously to exploit any pattern or relationship that seems to provide an insight into the future direction of the stock market. If the proverbial summer rally becomes perceived as a regular annual event, then investors will act to take advantage of it. How will they try to profit from an anticipated summer rally? By buying in the spring and selling in the summer, of course. What effect will this trading have on prices in the stock market? Obviously, heavy buying in the spring will push prices up and heavy selling in the summer will push prices down. The net effect is necessarily to diminish the strength of the summer rally and, ultimately, to erase it as a predictable move in the market. This logic suggests that any regular pattern in the stock market will tend to be eliminated by the collective effect of investors attempting to take advantage of it. Carrying this logic one step further, what movements remain in the stock market should be largely unpredictable or random. This is the essence of the random walk theory of the stock market that is taught these days to all MBA students. It says that future moves in the stock market cannot be forecasted from information that investors have today; stocks will go up or down, but which way or how far we cannot tell.

If I believed that the random walk theory was absolutely true I would not be writing this chapter. What I do believe is that there is no get-rich-quick formula for stock market timing. There is no alchemy for investors or economists any more than there is for chemists. If you were expecting to get rich by buying stocks in the spring and selling into the summer rally, forget it. The stock market has been analyzed thoroughly, using statistical methods designed to detect seasonal patterns (I have done a bit of this myself), and no reliable seasonal patterns emerge. It just can't be that easy. On the other hand, I have become convinced that relationships exist between certain economic indicators and the stock market which are persistent enough that they cannot be dismissed as illusion. As an academic economist and business school faculty member, I have been steeped in the strictest traditions of random walk orthodoxy. Like all logically sound theories it is not to be dismissed lightly. The burden is on those who would claim to demonstrate exceptions to it. Nevertheless, while doing research at the University of Chicago in the early 1970s on the response of the stock market to inflation, I was obliged to face the fact that the computer was telling me that changes in inflation signaled subsequent moves in the stock market. Let me show you, by means of charts, how this relationship seems to work.

We have looked before at the interaction of inflation and stock prices in Chapter 5. Let's take another look now from the viewpoint of timing—do changes in the rate of inflation signal changes in the direction of the stock market? Figure 33 shows inflation, measured as the percent change in the Consumer Price Index over the prior 12 months, as a solid line and the Standard & Poor's 500 Stock Index in inflation-adjusted or real terms as a dotted line. This real S&P 500 shows the purchasing power of a typical stock portfolio over time. Recall that the stock market peaked in real terms in the late 1960s, slid badly during most of the 1970s, and reached a bottom in 1982, at which point it had lost over 60 percent of the purchasing power it had at its peak. A good part of that loss has been recovered since 1982. Would inflation have helped us to see what was coming? Notice in the figure that the stock market seems to move in the opposite direction from inflation. Further, and more significantly, a major change in inflation generally preceded a move in the stock market in the opposite direction.

Inflation rose sharply in 1966 when stocks were at a peak and fell sharply in 1967 when the market was at a temporary low. When inflation heated up even more in 1968 and 1969, it was again time to dump stocks. In fact, it was a warning of serious trouble ahead, since stocks plunged in 1970 and never recovered the 1969 high. Inflation again receded in 1972 and the stock market continued its recovery until inflation heated up in 1973. An investor who unloaded in 1973 would have avoided much of the carnage of late 1973 and 1974. Inflation subsided in 1975, but this time there does not seem to have been a lag in the positive

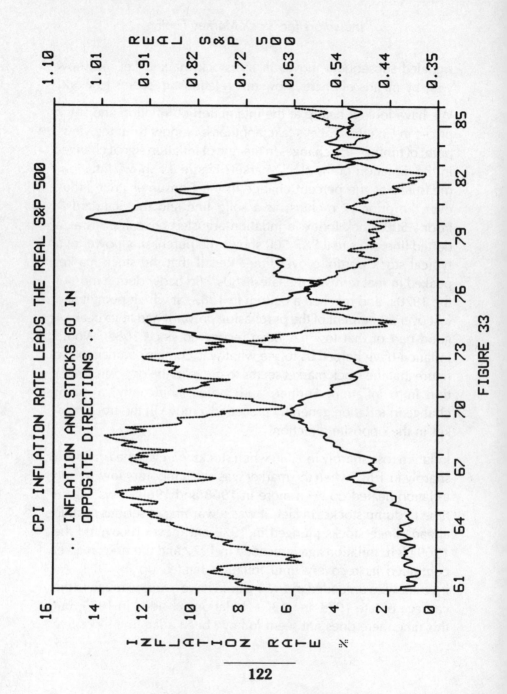

CPI INFLATION RATE LEADS THE REAL S&P 500

.. INFLATION AND STOCKS GO IN
OPPOSITE DIRECTIONS ..

FIGURE 33

response of the stock market. The next warning signal was given by inflation in early 1977, when the market was embarking on its big slide to the lows of 1982. Inflation started to give the next buy signal in 1981, a good year before the market bottom. The spectacular slide in the inflation rate back to 1960s levels by mid-1982 strongly suggested it was time to buy and hold stocks. The downward trend of inflation during 1984-1985 continued to suggest good times ahead for the stock market.

Why should there be an inverse relation between inflation and stocks? Without repeating the discussion of prior chapters, I think it is worth reiterating two major reasons. One is that when inflation heats up, it puts pressure on the Federal Reserve to take away the punch bowl, to put the brakes on the real economy in order to bring inflation back under control. This means poorer profits and higher interest rates which compete for the investor's dollar. The second major reason is that rising inflation has been a symptom of adverse developments in the real economy, such as the oil price shocks of the 1970s. Inflation is too many dollars chasing too few goods. It can be caused by too many dollars being created or by a reduction in the supply of goods in the real economy. Both are bad news for the stock market.

Based on our discussion of Figure 33, we can formulate a tentative trading rule: When inflation is on the rise, stay out of stocks; when it is on the decline, buy stocks. Let's see how this would have worked out if we measure the change in inflation from the corresponding month a year earlier. Figure 34 charts this measure of the change in inflation as the solid line, along with the real S&P 500 again as the dotted line. The horizontal line in the figure is zero change in inflation. When the solid line rises above the zero line, our rule tells us to sell stocks, and when it falls below to buy. The indicator is pretty much neutral until 1966 when it

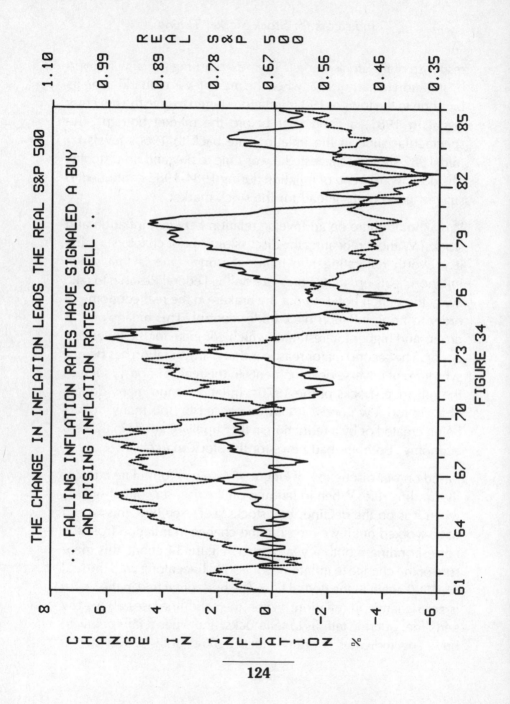

THE CHANGE IN INFLATION LEADS THE REAL S&P 500

.. FALLING INFLATION RATES HAVE SIGNALED A BUY
AND RISING INFLATION RATES A SELL ..

FIGURE 34

correctly signals a sell. The next clear sell signal is in 1968, again a good time to have unloaded. A clear buy signal in 1971 was a bit late to catch the full market recovery. By mid-1973 the indicator signaled sell, which would have saved the investor from the most severe market collapse on the chart, that of late 1973 and 1974. A clear buy signal was given in 1975, but again a bit late to catch the market rally. The sell signal of 1977 would have been most welcome, however. The indicator gave a buy signal in early 1981. This was a year early, but on the positive side, it did continue to give a very strong buy signal through the market lows of 1982. A brief sell signal in 1984 would have been modestly useful, and in 1985 the indicator returned to the buy side. This record suggests two things: that sell signals have been more reliable than buy signals and that leading indicators of inflation would help to improve the lead. That is why I read the commodities page very faithfully!

I have suggested that one reason why the inflation indicator works is that rising inflation triggers aggressive action by the Federal Reserve. This might explain why the indicator seems to work better as a sell signal. The Fed fights inflation by raising interest rates and stimulates a sagging economy by lowering interest rates. Recall also from Chapter 4 that there is an intimate relation between interest rates and inflation. This all points toward interest rates as another potential source of stock market timing indicators. Let's take a look at the yield on Treasury bills, our indicator of short term interest rates from Chapter 1, to see whether this might be the case. This indicator is charted in Figure 35 as the solid line along with the real S&P 500 index which will continue to be the dotted line. The immediate impression one

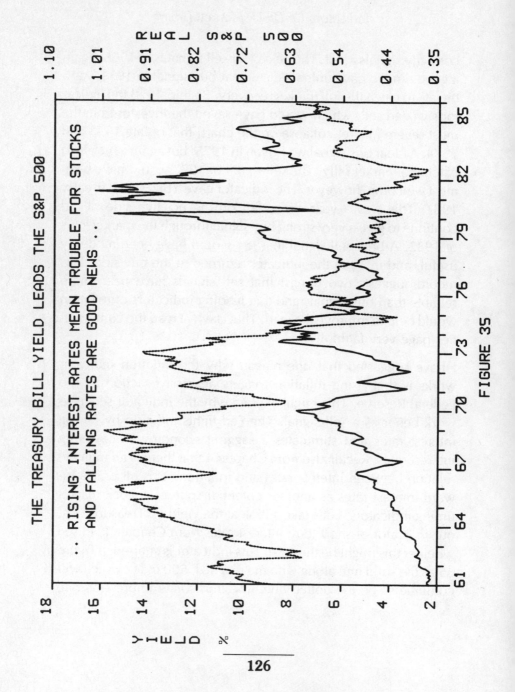

THE TREASURY BILL YIELD LEADS THE S&P 500

.. RISING INTEREST RATES MEAN TROUBLE FOR STOCKS
AND FALLING RATES ARE GOOD NEWS ..

FIGURE 35

gets from Figure 35 is that rising interest rates mean that trouble is ahead for the stock market, and falling rates are good news. Major market peaks have been preceded by rising short term interest rates and rallies have been accompanied by sharp declines in rates. Just as we did in the case of the inflation indicator, we are tempted to investigate the change in the Treasury bill rate, say, from the previous year's level, as a potential timing indicator. This is what we have in Figure 36.

The change in the Treasury bill rate from the previous year does not appear to have been a useful timing indicator until the 1967 minirecession. From late 1961 through 1965, the indicator, charted as the solid line, remained slightly above the zero level. We would be looking for a clear positive reading as a sell signal. This doesn't happen until late 1966 when the stock market had already slumped. We do see a buy signal, the indicator moving into negative territory, in early 1967 as the market is moving sharply higher. The indicator then moves to the sell side in 1968 and stays there as the market makes its historic peak and begins its plunge to the 1970 bottom. What is equally important is that it switches to the buy side just as that bottom is being reached. The next sell signal is in late 1972, just before the next major market peak.

Encouraging, to say the least! The indicator then gives a buy signal in early 1975 at the market bottom. A sell signal appears in the making in mid-1976 when the market reaches its next peak, but it is too weak to have warranted action. A clear sell signal develops in 1977, and the indicator stays on the sell side as the market drops lower into 1980. A brief buy signal accompanied the 1980 rally, then a strong sell at the 1980 peak. The indicator moves to the buy side starting in the fall of 1981 and continues to give stronger buy indications through the 1982 trough. The next

127

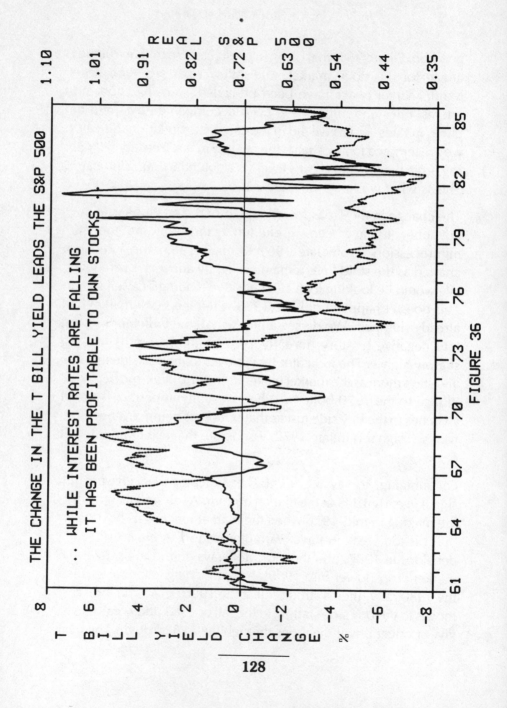

THE CHANGE IN THE T BILL YIELD LEADS THE S&P 500

.. WHILE INTEREST RATES ARE FALLING
IT HAS BEEN PROFITABLE TO OWN STOCKS

FIGURE 36

sell signal is in the fall of 1983 at the next market peak. Through 1985 the indicator stays clearly in buy territory. I don't know about you, but I am inclined to pay close attention to interest rates after seeing the record of this indicator as a market timer. That doesn't mean I'd bet the ranch on it (or on any other indicator) because it is not infallible. When it started to signal a buy in the fall of 1981, the market had another several months of disheartening decline ahead of it. You have to have had the financial reserves to ride out the rest of the storm and to take advantage of the continuing buying opportunity.

Another way to look at interest rates is in terms of the spread, or difference, between long and short term rates. When the Federal Reserve moves to stimulate the economy it pushes down short term rates faster than long term rates because, as we saw in Chapter 1, long term interest rates are more attuned to long-run factors in the economy. A positive spread then might be expected to signal an expanding economy. When the Fed sees that it is time to take away the punch bowl and sober up an overexuberant economy, it pushes interest rates up, but again, it will be short rates that respond more. A negative spread between long and short rates (long rates below short rates) should therefore be a signal of hard times ahead. Let's see whether the spread has been a useful indicator for stock market timing by looking at Figure 37 where it is charted as the solid line, along with the real S&P 500 as a dotted line. Indeed it appears that when the spread was positive it was often a good time to be holding stocks. The spread is positive until 1966 when the market hits an important peak. It then stays in negative territory (again, the horizontal line indicates zero for the indicator) from mid-1968 through mid-1970 while the market is in free fall. It turns positive at the 1970 market bottom and remains positive until the market starts its plunge to

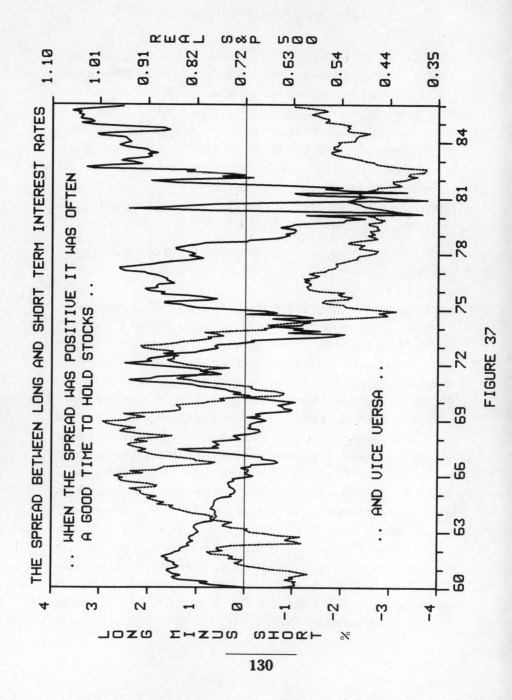

THE SPREAD BETWEEN LONG AND SHORT TERM INTEREST RATES

.. WHEN THE SPREAD WAS POSITIVE IT WAS OFTEN
A GOOD TIME TO HOLD STOCKS ..

... AND VICE VERSA ..

FIGURE 37

the 1974 low. By early 1975, the indicator has turned positive again and the market rallies. But then it starts to mislead us. While the market peaks in 1976 and begins its slide to the 1982 bottom, our indicator remains bullishly positive until the end of 1978. A brief buy signal in 1980 is probably too late to catch that rally. After another brief buy signal in early 1982, the spread turns solidly bullish in mid-1982 and remains bullish while the market soars. Not a bad record, I think, but clearly the indicator performs badly in the late 1970s, failing to get us out of the market during a serious decline.

Why does the spread indicator give a misleading signal in the late 1970s? I think the explanation lies in the relationship between interest rates and inflation that we discussed in Chapter 4. Interest rates tend to move up and down with inflation. If the money market sees rising inflation in the years ahead it will also expect higher interest rates. But recall from Chapter 1 that long term interest rates reflect the money market's forecast of future short term rates. Therefore, when long rates are above short rates (a positive spread) it may reflect rising inflation rather than an improving economy in the years ahead. This is very likely to have been the case in the late 1970s when inflation was accelerating and appeared to have gotten out of control. Inflation was much less of a factor in the 1960s and early 1970s. If I am right about this explanation, then the spread would be a more reliable indicator of the current dollar value of the stock market without adjustment for inflation. A positive spread could be suggesting a rising stock market either because the economy will be improving or because prices generally will be in an inflationary uptrend. Figure 38 charts the spread between the long term Treasury bond yield and the Treasury bill yield, which we saw before in Figure 4, against the S&P 500 without any adjustment of the index for

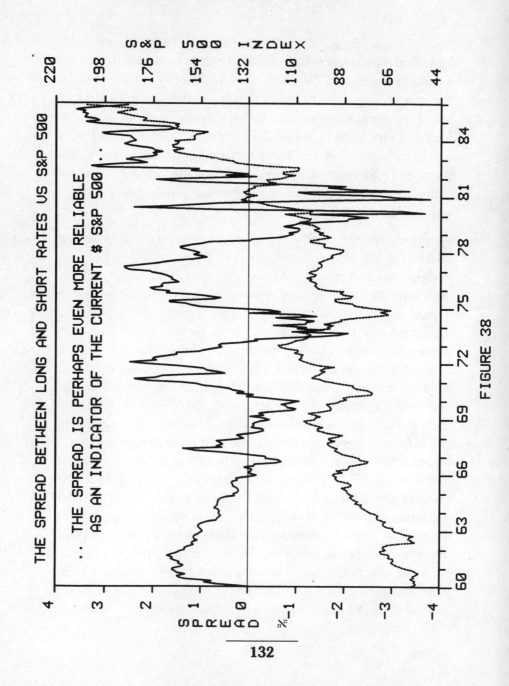

THE SPREAD BETWEEN LONG AND SHORT RATES VS S&P 500

... THE SPREAD IS PERHAPS EVEN MORE RELIABLE
AS AN INDICATOR OF THE CURRENT $ S&P 500...

FIGURE 38

132

inflation. We see that the 1975-1978 interval, when the spread was positive, was a good time for the stock market in current dollar terms. It rose sharply from the late 1974 low and held its level through 1978. Overall, the record of the indicator looks promising. It correctly signals the strength of the stock market in the first half of the 1960s and its fading vigor in the late 1960s. It produces a strong buy signal in late 1970 in time to ride the next major advance through 1972. Likewise, it gives a helpful buy signal in 1975. It then incorrectly signals a declining market in 1979, but does give a preview of the 1980 rally. It gives a good sell signal again in late 1980 and 1981, finally turning strongly and correctly to the buy side in 1982. The record suggests to me that the long-short interest rate spread is a very useful indicator of stock market direction as long as we keep in mind that it is an indicator of current dollar value—the values we see reported on the financial page—rather than inflation-adjusted real value.

Now that we have some timing indicators for the stock market, it is natural to consider how they might be improved. One direction for improvement is toward earlier warning of a change in market direction. We would have earlier warning if we detected a change in our indicator earlier. Perhaps we have been too conservative in measuring a change in inflation or interest rates as a change from the same month of the prior year. Maybe the change from six or three months earlier would be a more sensitive indicator. Readers who like to play with numbers and charts may want to experiment along these lines and discover a variant that works well for their style of investing. Home computers with user-friendly software make that kind of experimentation easier and quicker than ever. But be careful—a change in inflation or interest rates observed over a one- or two-month interval may be much less significant than one which is observed over a longer period.

133

Another strategy for developing more sensitive indicators is to look for leading indicators of stock market indicators. If inflation is a useful indicator for stock market timing, then a leading indicator of inflation should be even better. An obvious candidate comes out of our discussion of inflation in Chapter 2, namely, the Producer Price Index. Recall that the PPI measures prices at the manufacturing and wholesale levels before price changes have worked their way up to the level of the consumer. You may also recall or have noticed that the PPI is announced about a week before the CPI, sometimes a significant difference. Let's see whether we would have done better using the PPI as a market timing indicator by taking a look at Figure 39, where the change in the PPI inflation rate from a year earlier is shown by the solid line. As with the CPI, we would expect that a move in the indicator above the zero line would suggest trouble ahead for stocks, and declining inflation to indicate an improving environment for stocks. The PPI gave an earlier and stronger buy signal at the beginning of the 1967 rally, but started warning of the 1968 top at about the same time as the CPI. The PPI shows a slight edge at the 1970 low and gives earlier warning of inflation bubbling up in 1972 and early 1973, prior to the 1973 plunge in the market. It gives an earlier and clearer buy signal at the beginning of the 1975 rally. Similarly, it gives warning sooner of the rekindling of inflation in 1977 and the ensuing market slide. It is too early with a buy signal in late 1980 but continues to be strongly on the buy side through the 1982 bottom. Like the CPI, it gives probably too much encouragement to sell stocks in 1984 and persists past the 1984 trough, but it does switch to the buy side more quickly and convincingly in early 1985. Overall, I think that the PPI offers a bit of an edge in sensitivity over the CPI, but I watch both. As I mentioned earlier, I also watch commodity prices closely because they are even more current than the PPI. The Dow Jones

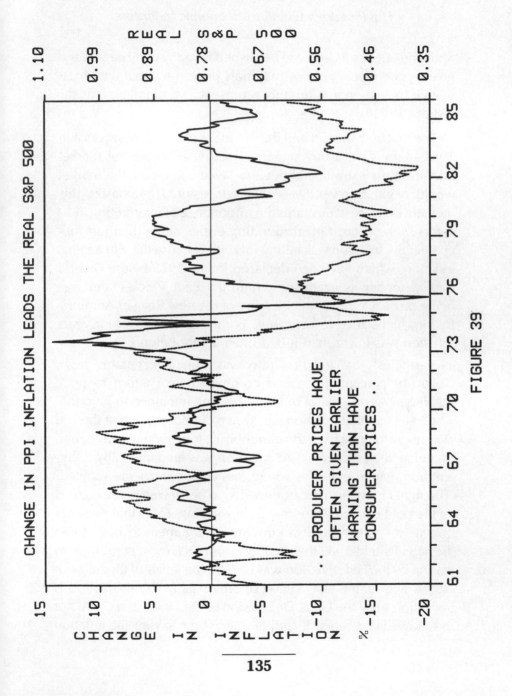

CHANGE IN PPI INFLATION LEADS THE REAL S&P 500

REAL S&P 500

1.10 0.99 0.89 0.78 0.67 0.56 0.46 0.35

.. PRODUCER PRICES HAVE
OFTEN GIVEN EARLIER
WARNING THAN HAVE
CONSUMER PRICES ..

FIGURE 39

CHANGE IN INFLATION

15 10 5 0 -5 -10 % -15 -20

Spot and Futures Indices are published in many daily papers and give a good reading of raw materials prices on a real time basis even if they are not as broadly representative of inflation as the PPI or the CPI.

Notice that both the CPI and the PPI made the same basic error in 1981—they gave a buy signal a good year before the market bottom. A very substantial decline lay ahead before the market would begin to reward a stalwart investor. I emphasize this incident because it illustrates the importance of interpreting indicators in the context of surrounding events rather than just mechanically. Inflation was falling in 1981 because the war against inflation, which had been declared in late 1979 by the Federal Reserve under its aggressive chairman Paul Volcker and was being prosecuted with the blessing of the new Reagan Administration, had started to bear fruit. For the first time in four years inflation was lower than it had been a year before.

Nevertheless, the inflation rate was still unacceptably high, about 10 percent, for a Fed committed to a return to price stability. A great deal of inflation fighting remained to be done. The mere fact that inflation was down did not mean that the Fed was ready to bring back the punchbowl, lower interest rates, and stimulate the economy. This situation was fundamentally different from earlier episodes where less drastic medicine sufficed. The signal from the indicator needed to be viewed in the context of the political and economic policy setting. From that perspective it was not by itself a convincing argument to buy stocks heavily. By mid-1982 the situation was much more conducive to easing by the Fed. Inflation was back to the levels of the halcyon 1960s and falling fast. The economy was in the most serious recession since the Great Depression of the 1930s and could not be allowed to deteriorate further. It was time to view the inflation indicators in a more favorable light and to heed the confirming evidence provided by falling interest rates and the rising long-short spread. The moral of the story is clear: Never trust any single indicator alone, and never adhere blindly to a mechanical rule for stock market trading.

The 1982 experience brings up another important rule of investing. Never become so heavily committed that you cannot afford to be wrong for a while. Even if your judgment is eventually proved right, there can often be a frustratingly long wait. If it is a longer wait than you expected, you can find yourself in the disastrous position of having used up your reserves and being forced out of the game before the payoff comes. This is what makes buying on margin (with borrowed money) so risky. If the market goes against you for a while, you may be unable, or unwilling, to continue to meet calls from your broker for more capital. A classic example of this was suffered by a group of my colleagues at the University of Chicago in 1969, and I was fortunate enough to be able to learn from their experience. They saw correctly that the Fed was trying to wring out some of the inflation that had been building up for two years. They noted that money supply growth was falling sharply and interest rates were shooting up. They correctly forecasted that when a recession got under way, the Fed would relent and that the result would be lower interest rates and, therefore, higher bond prices. Conclusion: Buy long term bonds on margin. This they did as a consortium and waited for the profits to roll in. Instead, what rolled in were margin calls. They were much too early and interest rates continued to skyrocket, bringing bond prices ever lower. After several rounds of margin calls, they had had enough. They threw in the towel and liquidated their position at a substantial loss. Of course that was just the point at which the market turned, and bonds subsequently rose sharply as the 1970 recession unfolded. Too late for the consortium; it was broke. You can be right about the long run trend and still get taken to the cleaners in the meantime.

Yet another strategy for sharpening our timing tools is to look at monetary variables which the Federal Reserve influences by its actions. In Chapter 9 we saw that the growth rate of the inflation-adjusted money supply (the M2 measure) was a powerful leading indicator of the real economy. Perhaps it is also useful as a barometer of the direction of the stock market. The reasoning is that the inflation-adjusted or real supply of money is a measure of the liquidity of the economy. When this liquidity measure is rising relatively rapidly, people will want to invest some of it in earning assets such as stocks. When liquidity is squeezed, as it is when the Fed is trying to put the brakes on inflation, then people are obliged to sell earning assets, including stocks, to try to maintain adequate liquidity to meet their financial obligations. This suggests that we look at the change in the growth rate of liquidity, say, over the past year. If this indicator is positive we would expect a rising stock market, and if it is negative we would expect stocks to take it on the chin. To check out whether it works, we take a look at Figure 40 where the change in the growth rate of real M2, our liquidity measure, is charted as the solid line, and the real S&P 500 as the usual dotted line.

It seems readily apparent from Figure 40 that changes in the growth rate of liquidity have anticipated major moves in the stock market. We are looking at dips of the liquidity indicator below the zero line as sell signals and moves above it as buy signals. The first sell signal is in early 1966, which anticipated the market decline. However, the liquidity indicator does not swing back to the plus side in time to tip us off to the 1967 rally. The strong sell

CHANGE IN THE GROWTH OF REAL M2 LEADS REAL S&P 500

.. CHANGES IN THE GROWTH RATE OF LIQUIDITY HAVE
ANTICIPATED MAJOR MOVES IN THE STOCK MARKET ..

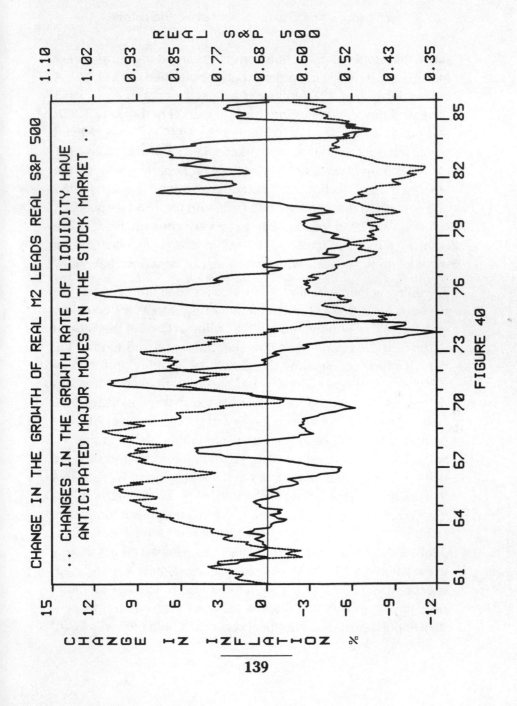

FIGURE 40

signal that started in late 1968 correctly warned of a serious bear market, and it persisted until the market bottomed out in 1970. A buy signal in late 1970 followed by a sell signal in early 1973 were well timed to get us into the bull market of the early 1970s and out of it in time to avoid the 1973–1974 collapse. Next it would have gotten us into the market in 1975 and out in late 1977 for little, if any, net gain. The sell signal persisted through the ensuing market decline until a buy signal emerged in early 1981 and continued through the 1982 nadir and the 1983 recovery. A sell signal in 1984 was too late to be very constructive, but we were back in the market in 1985. All in all a pretty encouraging record, I think, and one which warrants our continued attention.

The unifying theme behind all the stock market timing indicators we have looked at is the interaction of the monetary economy with the real economy through the policy actions of the Federal Reserve. If the economy is in a slump the Fed will tend to cut interest rates, accelerating the growth of liquidity and thereby stimulating the real economy and the stock market. When this process has continued for a time we see that inflation tends to heat up, putting pressure on the Fed to go into reverse. At some point inflation will be regarded as intolerably high and the Fed will act to push interest rates up, contract liquidity, and slow the real economy which leads to a stock market slump. Is it possible that politics and the timing of elections plays an important role in this cycle? How cynical of me even to suggest it! But look at the evidence. The stock market rose sharply in 1952, 1960, 1964, 1968, 1972, 1976 (sort of), and 1980 and at least it rallied sharply in the summer of 1984. All Presidential election years. The clear exception is 1956. I guess we liked Ike so much that he didn't need any help. But, you say, the Federal Reserve is an independent entity free of direct political control. Would the Fed's Board of Governors stoop to playing politics? You bet they would. Consider the hasty and ill-conceived credit controls the Fed slapped on the economy in the spring of 1980 at the request of a panicky Carter Administration that was grabbing at straws in a last ditch attempt to halt runaway inflation before November. The Fed subserviently obliged, and the result was a completely unnecessary recession—and, ironically, the defeat of President Carter. I just cannot imagine the Fed having engaged in such an extreme (and foolhardy) action without the time pressure of a fall election.

The Bottom Line

The experience of the past quarter century suggests that indicators based on shifts in the rate of inflation, interest rates, the spread between long and short term interest rates, and the growth rate of real M2 can be useful in signaling the direction of the stock market. Their effectiveness seems to be related to the political-economic cycle of monetary policy. But no indicator is infallible, and they all need to be interpreted in the context of current economic and political developments. Never take a position that leaves you without the reserves to ride out a storm. Many is the investor (and economist) whose judgment was vindicated in the long run but who went bust in the short run.

11

That Scary Federal Deficit: Will We Ever Get Rid of It?

It is one of the great ironies of politics that record-breaking budget deficits have occurred during the most conservative administration since Herbert Hoover. From a position of near-balance in 1979, the deficit of the U.S. government exploded to well over $200 billion in 1982 and by the end of 1985 showed no sign of turning around. The situation is graphically evident in Figure 41 where negative readings indicate a deficit and positive readings a surplus. The federal budget seems to have fallen off a cliff. This is surely one of the most perplexing and disquieting developments of the decade, and many have come to despair of ever seeing a solution. In arithmetic terms the problem is simple—the government spends vastly more than it receives in taxes. In 1985, it collected about $800 billion in tax revenue but spent about $1000 billion (yes, that is one TRILLION dollars). Tax revenues have grown, but spending has grown faster. In order to have the cash to pay its bills, the U.S. Treasury sells bills, notes, and

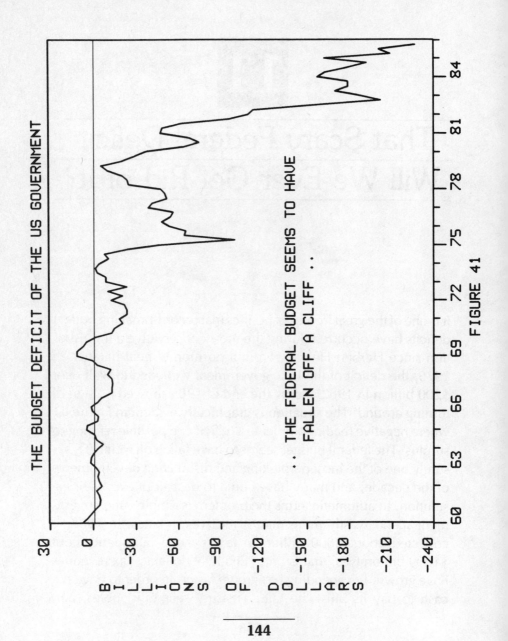

THE BUDGET DEFICIT OF THE US GOVERNMENT

... THE FEDERAL BUDGET SEEMS TO HAVE
FALLEN OFF A CLIFF ..

FIGURE 41

bonds. The outstanding total of these securities is the federal debt, often called the national debt. By the end of 1985, the federal debt was about $2000 billion (two trillion dollars) and growing at the rate of $200 billion per year. These are staggering numbers, and it is important to look at them in perspective if we are to see how serious the problem is, how we got here, what the consequences are for the economy, and what our chances are for a long term solution.

You haven't read this far in the book without knowing that inflation has distorted everything that is measured in dollars. To be able to say how much bigger the deficit *really* was in 1985 than it was 10 or 20 years earlier, we need to adjust it by the amount of inflation that has occurred. When the deficit is expressed in constant 1982 dollars we get the picture shown in Figure 42. Now we can start to see some relationships that make sense. Notice that the deficit always grows (a larger negative reading on the chart) during a recession: 1967, 1970–1971, 1974–1975, 1980, and 1981–1982 were all periods when the deficit widened. This is not surprising. When a recession develops, the government's tax collections fall. Shrinking incomes and plummeting profits reduce the tax base. Spending does not shrink in a recession, though; it tends to rise instead, because more people qualify for welfare programs such as unemployment insurance and Aid to Families with Dependent Children. Accordingly, the 1982 deficit was about as bad as the 1975 deficit, since the 1981–1982 recession was about as severe as the 1974–1975 recession. When a recession ends and incomes rise again, the government collects more taxes, people leave the welfare rolls, and the budget moves back toward balance. Notice that the government ran a modest surplus in 1969 and nearly balanced the budget in 1973 and 1979. These were years of

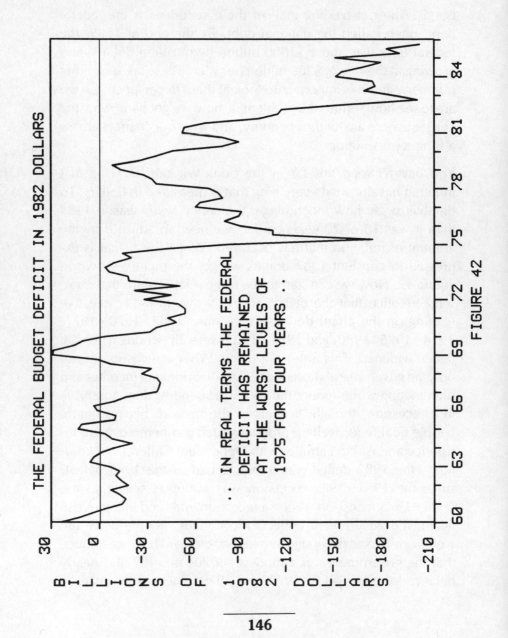

THE FEDERAL BUDGET DEFICIT IN 1982 DOLLARS

.. IN REAL TERMS THE FEDERAL
DEFICIT HAS REMAINED
AT THE WORST LEVELS OF
1975 FOR FOUR YEARS ..

FIGURE 42

prosperity. But something went haywire after 1982. The economy experienced a recovery in 1983 which carried on into 1984
and 1985, but the the federal budget did not. Contrary to the
traditional pattern, the deficit stayed at deep recession levels for
four years. At the end of 1985 it showed little, if any, evidence of
improvement.

We want to be careful that we are not being fooled into a Chicken
Little reaction by the fact that we are dealing with a growing
economy. The real economy was much larger in the 1980s than it
was in the 1960s. A moderate deficit will be much larger, even in
constant dollars, in a large economy than in a small one. A simple
way to correct for growth is to measure the deficit as a percent of
Gross National Product (GNP). This is shown in Figure 43. Notice that deficits, and occasional surpluses, amounted to only 1 or
2 percent of GNP until 1975, when the deficit briefly exceeded 6
percent of GNP. The 1982 deficit, viewed in this perspective,
was only about as bad as the 1975 deficit, again reflecting the fact
that those were comparable recession years. But after 1982 the
deficit seems to be stuck at about 5 percent of GNP. This is
unprecedented in peacetime U.S. history. It is also a staggering
number in itself. The spending of the federal government is
exceeding its income by an amount equal to 5 percent of the total
income of the entire society. To put it another way, the federal
debt is piling up at a rate equal to 5 percent of our national
income each year. Clearly this is a situation that cannot go on
forever.

How have we gotten into this situation? What is different about
the mid-1980s that has so completely upset past relationships
between federal income and spending? One obvious culprit is
the lackluster performance of the real economy that was docu-
mented in Chapter 6. Yes, there was a recovery from the 1982

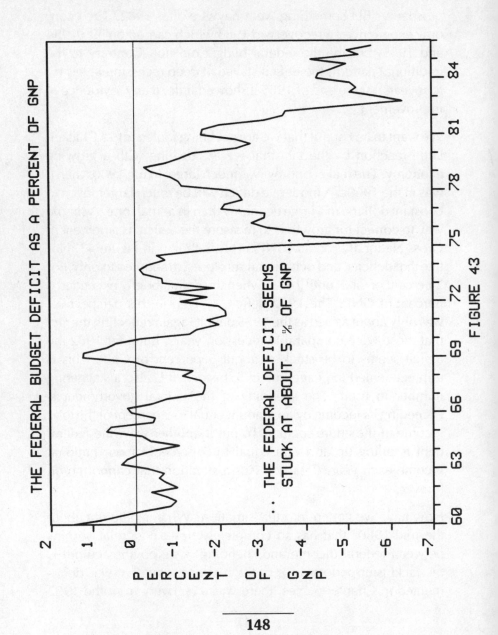

THE FEDERAL BUDGET DEFICIT AS A PERCENT OF GNP

... THE FEDERAL DEFICIT SEEMS
STUCK AT ABOUT 5 % OF GNP ...

FIGURE 43

recession lows, but that recession had come on the heels of the 1980 recession without time for a full recovery. Remember that the 1979 peak in Industrial Production was only attained again in 1983, making for four years without real growth. While the recovery did continue in 1984 and 1985, it proceeded at a modest pace and Capacity Utilization never got back to its 1979 levels, much less to the levels of the 1960s. Perhaps we are seeing recession level deficits because we never really recovered from the past two recessions. To try to see how far this explanation can go toward resolving the mystery, we compare the deficit as a percent of GNP (the solid line), to the rate of Capacity Utilization (the dotted line) in Figure 44. What we see is that the recovery in the economy following the 1982 low far outpaced the recovery of the federal budget. During the 1970s the condition of the budget closely reflected the condition of the economy, as revealed by the close correspondence of the two lines in the figure. When the economy slumped, the deficit worsened in lock step, and when it recovered, the deficit shrank at the same pace. This held true when the economy deteriorated from the 1979 peak, but then the deficit simply failed to follow along during the recovery of 1983–1985. The fact that the recovery did not carry the economy on to new heights cannot therefore by itself explain the persistence of the deficit.

Why then did the deficit fall out of step with the economy? The answer is clearly that the Economic Recovery Tax Act of 1981 reduced the federal government's take out of the national income. ERTA enacted sweeping reductions in both personal and corporate taxes and provided for the indexation of tax brackets to future inflation (more about indexation and what it means later). The top personal rate fell from 70 percent to 50 percent and individual income taxes were cut about 23 percent over a three-

149

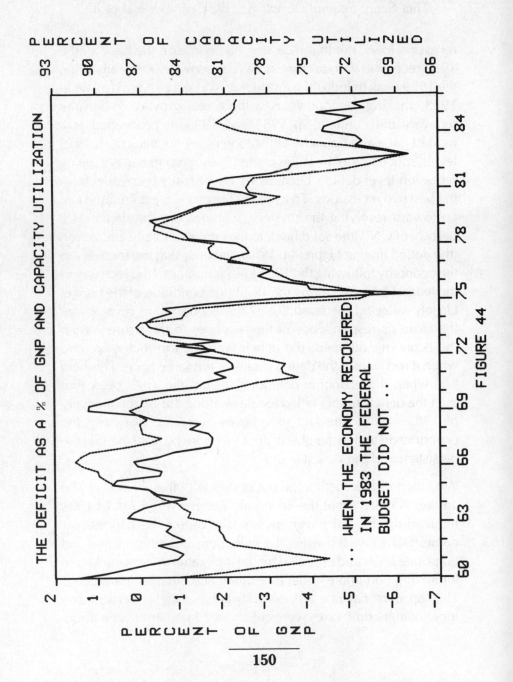

PERCENT OF CAPACITY UTILIZED

THE DEFICIT AS A % OF GNP AND CAPACITY UTILIZATION

.. WHEN THE ECONOMY RECOVERED
IN 1983 THE FEDERAL
BUDGET DID NOT ..

FIGURE 44

PERCENT OF GNP

year period. Eligibility for IRA plans was widened to include those covered by employer-sponsored retirement plans and the allowable contribution was raised from $1500 to $2000. ERTA also allowed business to write off new assets faster and expanded the system of tax credits for capital investments. The net effect was to cut the federal government's share of GNP from over 21 percent in 1981 to under 20 percent in 1985. If federal spending had also been reduced as a percentage of GNP, then we could have had the tax cut without a rise in the deficit. A reduction in federal spending as a percentage of GNP could be achieved in either of two ways: Spending in dollar terms could have been slashed, or the economy would have to grow more rapidly than federal spending. Congress took no steps in 1981 to cut dollar spending. Instead, the theory was that the economy would grow at an exceptionally rapid pace during the next few years, causing revenues to rise faster and reducing spending as a percentage of GNP. This was the *supply-side theory* of federal finance.

The basic idea behind the supply-side theory is that taxation discourages economic activity. Imagine, for the sake of illustration, that the government puts a tax on chocolate bars. If the tax is small, say, 1 percent of the price, it will have little adverse effect on the sales of chocolate bars, and the amount of tax collected will be about 1 percent of the amount previously spent on chocolate bars. Now suppose that the tax rate is increased in steps each year. At some point, chocolate bars become so expensive that only the most hopeless of chocolate freaks are still buying them. Lower sales volume starts to offset the higher tax rate until further tax rate increases have the effect of reducing the amount of tax collected. If the tax is high enough, say, 1000 percent, no bars will be sold at all, and the tax collected will be zero. Clearly a tax can be so high as to reduce the revenue collected, and when this is the case a tax cut will actually increase the amount of tax revenue. My freshman economics teacher gave as an example of this the reduction in Italy's very high gasoline taxes after World War II. To everyone's surprise, gas tax collections rose instead of fell because people bought much more gas.

The same idea is applied by the supply-siders to income taxes. As income tax rates rise, people are discouraged from working harder and from taking business risks. Why put in that extra effort if a possible raise in salary will be taxed away at a 70 percent rate? Why save to invest in risky business ventures if Uncle Sam will cut himself in for half of the profits? The income tax burden can reach a point where a tax rate increase will reduce tax revenues, but a tax cut will increase them because the tax cut will give people the incentive to raise their incomes. Work effort, investment, and risk-taking are the supply-side of the economy; increase these and you have a larger pie to slice. These principles were not new with the supply-siders, nor were they controversial with the majority of economists. In fact, many mainstream economists had been warning for many years that our tax system was having a negative impact on the economy because of disincentives to save, invest, and work. What was new and controversial in the supply-siders' position was the contention that our tax rates had escalated to the point where the revenue lost from a tax cut would actually be made up by a resulting higher GNP.

Who turned out to be right, the supply-siders or the mainstream economists? If the supply-siders had been right, we would have had a spectacular rise in the real economy after 1981. Tax revenues, a smaller share of a much larger pie, would have risen, and the deficit would have been wiped out. Unfortunately this did not happen. As we have seen, the real economy managed only a lackluster performance following the tax cut. If anything, the recovery from the 1981–1982 recession was below par. This does not mean that the 1981 tax cut had no beneficial effects on the economy, indeed my personal view is that those cuts were highly constructive. There is no doubt in my mind that a 70 percent tax creates a severe distortion of the incentives for economic effort. I also do not doubt that some of the tax cut will be recovered over time by the stimulus that a lower tax structure provides. It is impossible, in my experience, to visit countries which have very high tax rates without coming away with the conviction that they are shooting themselves in the foot and that their economies bear witness to the damage. But the U.S. economy in 1981 was not at a point where a tax cut would boost tax revenues, nor should anyone with common sense have thought it was.

If the supply-siders' position was too extreme to be plausible, why was it so persuasive to Congress and the public? In my view it provided the sugar-coating on the pill. The new administration wanted to ease the tax burden on the economy, but the problem was how to sell it without spending cuts. Republicans have always put a high priority on balancing the federal budget. Sizable spending cuts were out of the question because the new administration was committed to building up the armed forces. Social security was untouchable, partly because the inflation of the prior several years had devastated the savings of many elderly Americans and left them in desperate financial straits. But if a tax cut would actually *increase* revenue instead of *reduce* it, then *voilà*! no problem. We get to have our cake and eat it, too! Now the American people are not stupid, and even our politicians realize that you rarely get something for nothing. This supply-side theory was going to take some real selling, but that is something we are better at than anyone.

If Arthur Laffer hadn't existed he would have to have been invented. Almost single-handedly, Laffer articulated the supply-side position and sold it to the press and to the economists advising the President. He is certainly the most persuasive economist since Keynes. Keynes helped people believe that more government was better government at a time when that was what they wanted to believe. Laffer helped people believe that lower taxes would produce more tax revenue at a time when that was what they wanted to believe. An effective marketing campaign needs a good logo, and Laffer provided that with the famous Laffer curve. There was even a good story to go with it and a bit of legend never hurts. Laffer was explaining the supply-side idea to a *Wall Street Journal* editor, and to get the point across (journalism and economics don't seem to mix well) he drew an arch on a cocktail napkin. The arch represented the level of tax revenues over a range of tax rates. Revenues would be zero if the tax rate were zero, revenues would rise as the tax rate increased, then revenues would reach a maximum after which point a further increase in the tax rate would reduce revenues until again they were zero. The Laffer curve was the Golden Arch of the supply-side revolution and proved every bit as effective a marketing tool as those other Golden Arches. It got the point across and seemed to give the whole campaign a scientific basis. Mathematical curves serve the same purpose for the economics profession that Latin names do for the medical profession. When you go to the doctor with a complaint you usually get a translation of your words into Latin and sometimes little else. But that is very valuable (it must be, because we pay a lot for it) since it leads us to believe that we have consulted someone who has much more scientific knowledge on the subject than we do. Similarly, the economist's ability to translate sometimes simple ideas into mathematical curves or formulas gives us the assurance that there is a sound scientific basis for his or her theory. The catch with the Laffer curve was that whether a tax cut would increase revenue or reduce it depended on just where we were on that curve in 1981. Analysis by reputable scholars suggested that there was very little chance that we were anywhere near the downhill section of the curve; a tax cut would almost certainly reduce government revenues and increase the budget deficit. But no matter, the country wanted that tax cut, and a temporary suspension of disbelief is a small price to pay for a good night's sleep. Hardly a week went by without a strident editorial in the *Wall Street Journal* extolling the impeccable logic of the supply-side position and ridiculing any doubting Thomas. Contrary opinion prevailed in the economics profession, but little ink was wasted on such nay-sayers. We were not about to be put off that tax cut by warnings of big deficits from practitioners of the dismal science.

Arthur Laffer's prodigious powers of persuasion were no surprise to those of us who knew him professionally. As an assistant professor at the University of Chicago in the late 1960s he had taken the place by storm. I remember him as a short, stout young fellow with a shock of unruly light brown hair who appeared to bounce with boundless energy. He talked a mile a minute and seemed to be able to convince anyone of anything. If he had said that 2 plus 2 equals 5, the ensuing debate would convince you that you had somehow been wrong all these years. His skill as debater was rivaled only by that of his famous colleague, Milton Friedman. The University of Chicago is one of our most distinguished universities, and ordinary mortals slave for several years turning out scholarly tomes before being considered for tenure there. Laffer was granted tenure after only one year in residence, probably an all-time record. Such was the awe that Laffer inspired in his senior colleagues. Little wonder that ten years later he was able to convince the nation that it could have the same level of government services and pay less for it.

The effects that the deficit has had on the U.S. economy are the subject of a heated debate among economists that so far has failed to produce a consensus. Common sense suggests to most people that a higher deficit will push up interest rates and keep them higher than they would be otherwise. This is also the position held by the majority of professional economists. The reasoning goes like this: A $200 billion deficit is $200 billion that the government has to come up with somehow to pay its bills. Like any of us would have to, it borrows. The U.S. Treasury sells bills, notes, and bonds on the open market in competition with private borrowers. These securities are purchased by banks, insurance companies, mutual funds, pension funds, households, and foreign investors. Other borrowers are also trying to sell securities to these same lenders. What will induce them to buy an additional $200 billion of securities each year? A higher rate of return, of course. Instead of offering to pay 5 percent, borrowers may need to offer 10 percent or more. Some borrowers will fall by the wayside, unwilling or unable to pay higher interest rates. Some new houses will not be built because of higher mortgage costs. Some autos will not be purchased because of higher consumer loan rates. Some factories will not be built because of the higher cost of corporate debt. This is the mechanism by which resources are transferred from private use to government use. Instead of giving up purchasing power to the government entirely through taxes, the private sector is forced also to surrender purchasing power by the higher interest costs it now faces. As long as spending by the government is not cut, it will get its purchasing power one way or the other. This is called "crowding out." The lesson here is that the true burden of government is not measured simply by the tax revenue it collects but by its spending. Only a reduction in spending can reduce that burden.

When we talk about higher interest cost here we mean, of course, *real interest* as we defined it in Chapter 5. Recall that the real interest rate is the quoted rate less the rate of inflation. If mortgage rates rise by 2 percentage points but inflation accelerates by the same amount, then the real cost of the mortgage is unchanged. The home owner will be compensated for higher interest payments by the more rapid appreciation of the house. It is a higher real interest rate on mortgages that discourages home building. Similarly, it is only a higher real interest rate which induces investors to absorb the additional securities being sold by the Treasury. We saw in Chapter 5 that real interest rates have been much higher in the 1980s than they were before. While nominal interest rates as quoted on the financial page did fall from the 1981 peak, real interest rates stayed at record high levels. To many economists this is evidence of the crowding-out effect of the deficit.

But there is another reason why real interest rates have been high, namely, the Federal Reserve's war against inflation. Remember that in late 1979 the Fed made a major turnabout in monetary policy, shifting from a policy aimed at keeping interest rates low to one of bringing down inflation by slowing the growth rate of the money supply. In Chapter 4 we discussed how this would push up real interest rates and the role that higher rates play in fighting inflation. Indeed it was in 1980 that interest rates shot up, not in 1982–1983 when the ERTA tax cuts took effect. On the other hand, maybe the credit markets were smart enough to see that tax cut and resulting higher deficit coming down the road. Now you know why there are so many two-handed economists, a characteristic that President Harry Truman pointed out in frustration to his advisors. There is often more than one good explanation for an economic event, and this is a classic example. Economists call this the *identification problem*, and it plagues the science.

There is even a significant school of thought in the profession that argues the seemingly ridiculous position that the deficit will have *no* effect on the level of interest rates. It depends on the notion that taxpayers realize that sooner or later they will have to pay for government spending. A government deficit only pushes those inevitable taxes into the future. Forward-looking individuals will make provision for those future taxes in their own budgets, setting aside enough to cover their share of the government deficit. If they do their arithmetic right, the additional savings put aside by taxpayers will be just enough to finance the government deficit with no change in interest rates. Their reduced personal spending makes just the right amount of resources available to the government. Whether you believe this story or not, it is an ingenious one, and it is not new. It was first put forward by the great English economist David Ricardo, who wrote in the decades around 1800. Ricardo had no formal university training but took up the subject after making a large fortune in business by the age of 30. Several of the most important ideas used in economics today are due to Ricardo. Ricardo's theory that deficits need not change interest rates is most plausible for a temporary deficit that will clearly be paid off in the foreseeable future. Debt incurred by the British Crown during the Napoleonic Wars of Ricardo's time might be a good example. Much of the academic debate surrounding the applicability of Ricardo's theory to our present situation involves the question of whether our federal debt will ever be paid off and whether individuals look far enough into the future to make provision for an eventual tax liability.

What do I believe? I think it is important not to pretend to know more than we really do. In my view there is ample historical evidence that an anti-inflation monetary policy such as we had after 1979 will push interest rates up in real terms. There is some convincing historical research which suggests that deficits have not pushed interest rates up as much as the commonsense argument would imply. But the early 1980s were unique in that we were confronted with inflation and deficits that were unprecedented in peacetime U.S. experience. I suspect that the inflation will have largely disappeared well before the deficit problem is solved, and this should give us a better handle on their separate effects.

There is one effect that many people expected the deficit to have that it did *not* have. The deficit was supposed to make inflation worse, in the view of a substantial fraction of academic and business economists, as well as noneconomists. In talking with individual investors, this is a fear I frequently hear expressed. I am sure that this is one reason why the decline of inflation since 1981 has come as a surprise to so many people. Conventional wisdom said that when the government spends more than it takes in, you have more money chasing the same amount of goods, so prices will be bid up as consumers—flush with their tax cuts—compete with the government for available goods. Many people seem to believe that the government "runs the printing press" to cover the deficit as do governments of many third world nations. This last point about creating money is really separate from the first point, although they are often confused. The tax cut will indeed add to the total demand for goods in the economy unless David Ricardo was right about people saving their money in anticipation of the deficit. This would put upward pressure on prices if the economy were already perking along at something near capacity. But of course in 1981 it wasn't. Instead, there was considerable unused capacity throughout the world economy that was ready and able to satisfy growing demand following the deep recession of 1981 – 1982. Furthermore, the deficit was not financed by running the printing press as it has been in highly inflationary economies like Brazil or Israel. Instead, it was financed primarily by selling Treasury securities in competition with private borrowers.

In our monetary system the Treasury does not have discretion to print money at will. If the securities issued by the Treasury to cover the deficit had been bought by the Federal Reserve, then the effect would undoubtedly have been highly inflationary. This is because when the Fed buys Treasury securities it creates new money in the banking system (see Chapter 3). It puts in an order to buy with a dealer in government securities, just as any buyer would. The difference comes in how payment is made. The Fed simply credits the account of the bank representing the dealer since the Fed acts like the bank's bank. How can it do this? It simply has the legal authority to do so. This credit in the bank's account at the Fed is money that did not exist before, and it becomes money in the bank just like the money in any bank account. That is the Fed's "printing press." While the Treasury was running up its big debt during the first half of the 1980s, the Fed was buying only about 10 percent of it. The Fed was willing to see interest rates shoot up during the early 1980s rather than finance the deficit by using its printing press because it knew that this was the only way inflation could be brought under control. A government deficit need not be inflationary. Whether it is or not depends on how it is financed. But will the Fed be able to stick to this discipline in the future when inflation-fighting has ceased to be the top priority and political pressure mounts for lower interest rates? With the war against inflation largely successful, but the economy less than vibrant in the mid-1980s, the Fed will undoubtedly feel the pressure to help bail out the Treasury by buying more of its debt. This is the specter a continuing deficit raises for the future. We need to keep a close watch on the Fed in the years ahead for signs that its resolve is weakening. If that happens, then we are in for a new era of inflation.

What are the prospects for eliminating, or at least drastically narrowing, the federal deficit in the years ahead? One kind of answer would point to the Gramm-Rudman-Hollings legislation, which mandates gradual reduction of the deficit, and say that the long term problem is solved. But I think it is naive to think that the GRH will force Congress to take actions that are politically unacceptable. If it comes to that, Congress will change the law or plead exemption under some pretext or other. The fundamental nature of the problem facing Congress is evident in Figure 45 which shows federal spending (solid line) and federal revenues (dotted line) as a percentage of GNP, which is the best measure we have of the nation's total income. While federal spending has continued to represent an ever-larger share of the nation's income, tax revenues have remained a fairly stable fraction of it. By the end of 1985 the gap had widened to about 5 percent of GNP. This is not an imbalance that can be rectified by some minor adjustments in the tax code or by ending a few small programs. The upward trend in spending has been no less evident since 1980 than in the past. Spending, of course, surged as a percent-

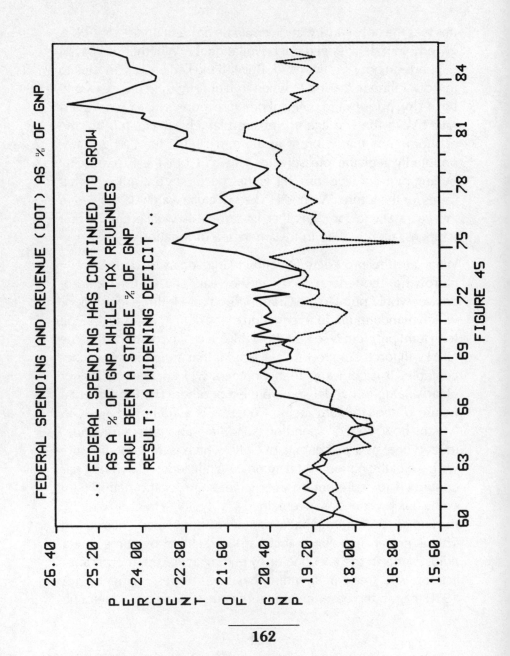

FEDERAL SPENDING AND REVENUE (DOT) AS % OF GNP

.. FEDERAL SPENDING HAS CONTINUED TO GROW
AS A % OF GNP WHILE TAX REVENUES
HAVE BEEN A STABLE % OF GNP
RESULT: A WIDENING DEFICIT ..

FIGURE 45

age of GNP during the 1981–1982 recession and then fell back as the economy recovered. But the upward trend reasserted itself as the economy returned to normal in 1984 and 1985. This figure also helps to put the 1981 tax cut in more meaningful perspective. As you can see, tax revenues have averaged about 20 percent of GNP since 1960. They had crept upward significantly after the 1975 recession and reached a peak in 1981 before ERTA took effect. That upward creep was due to the effect that the inflation of the late 1970s had on both personal and business tax rates.

In 1975 a married couple with taxable income of $20,000 was in the 32 percent marginal tax bracket (the rate of taxation on the incremental dollar of income) and paid 22 percent of their income to Uncle Sam. By 1981 inflation had raised the cost of living by about 70 percent, so this same couple needed an income of about $34,000 to keep up the same pretax real income. But because the tax tables were not adjusted for inflation, they would have been pushed up into the 37 percent marginal tax bracket where they would pay 23 percent of their income to Uncle Sam. In Chapter 7 we saw how inflation puffed up the accounting profits of corporations because it caused depreciation expense and cost of goods sold to be understated. The tax paid on these nonexistent profits was very real and caused corporate tax collections to increase rapidly from 1975 to 1981. Inflation was a powerful engine of taxation for the federal government, allowing it to raise its share of society's income without legislation. ERTA in effect adjusted tax rates for the inflation that had occurred in the 1970s, but it also indexed tax brackets in the future. This means that the dollar income level at which each tax rate takes effect would be adjusted annually according to the amount of inflation which had occurred. Our hypothetical couple would not be pushed into higher tax brackets again simply because of inflation. Corporations got significantly faster depreciation schedules to compensate for the previous bias in the tax code. The federal government could not depend on inflation to increase its take surreptitiously as it had in the 1970s. Now if Congress is to tackle the basic problem it must either halt the tendency of spending to grow faster than the economy, or raise taxes significantly.

Many people still think of the federal government primarily as the provider of national defense, postal service, parks, advice on when to plant crops, and space exploration. Actually, the main activity of the federal government these days is to put money in people's pockets. These are called transfer payments. They are transfers from taxpayers to groups that qualify for these payments. This includes Social Security, Medicare, Medicaid, and welfare payments. To see how transfer payments have come to dominate federal spending, let's take a look at Figure 46 where some broad categories of spending are charted as a percentage of GNP. The traditional functions of government are covered under the broad heading of "goods and services." In the 1960s this amounted to about 11 percent of GNP but by the mid-1970s had shrunk to about 8 percent. A big part of goods and services is, of course, national defense, the dotted line in Figure 46. We see that the decline of goods and services from the 1960s to the 1970s was basically due to the declining defense budget after Vietnam. National defense as a fraction of GNP fell from a high of 9 percent to a low of about 5 percent. The defense build-up that started in the late 1970s pushed that fraction back up to over 6 percent, and this is mirrored in a corresponding rise in goods and services. But there is no general upward trend here that would account for the upward trend in total spending.

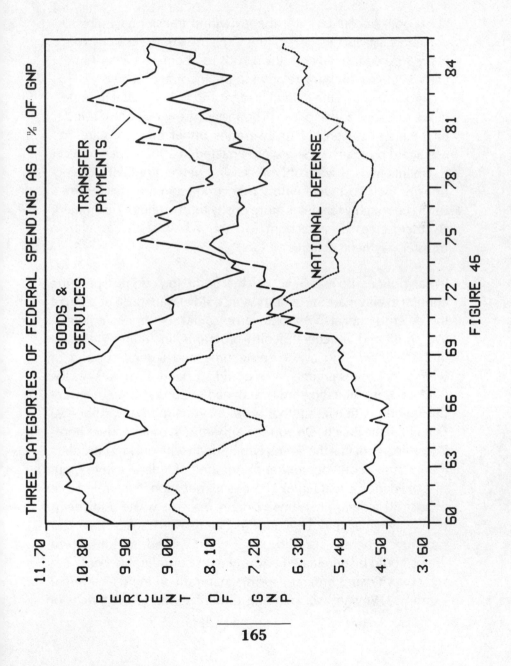

THREE CATEGORIES OF FEDERAL SPENDING AS A % OF GNP

GOODS & SERVICES

TRANSFER PAYMENTS

NATIONAL DEFENSE

FIGURE 46

PERCENT OF GNP

11.70 10.80 9.90 9.00 8.10 7.20 6.30 5.40 4.50 3.60

60   63   66   69   72   75   78   81   84

What does account for it is the growth in transfer payments. As you can see from the dashed line in Figure 46, these went from a mere 5 percent of GNP in the 1960s to about 10 percent in the early 1980s, a doubling relative to the income of society. This is the growth area of the federal budget and is now equal in importance to goods and services. The fastest growing part of transfer payments has been health insurance under the Medicare and Medicaid programs. These were enacted in 1965, when transfer payments in total were only about 4.5 percent of GNP. Projections of their cost were wildly inaccurate and they have turned out to be roughly ten times more costly than originally estimated. By themselves they account for about half of the growth in transfer payments relative to GNP.

What options do we have at this point for cutting spending enough to eliminate the deficit? We could eliminate 80 percent of the defense budget. We could drop social security completely. We could end all federal health programs, including Medicare and Medicaid, and at the same time end federal support of welfare programs entirely. We could suspend payments on the national debt (imitating the threatened action of some bankrupt third world nations), but that would take care of only about 70 percent of the deficit. Do you see any attractive alternatives here? The point is not that the deficit can be dealt with only by complete elimination of one or another major area of federal activity, but that the deficit is that large. There is no question in my mind that almost all federal programs contain massive waste and inefficiency whether they be national defense or transfer payment programs. There is also little doubt in my mind that some programs could be eliminated entirely with considerable benefit to society. The farm program springs naturally to mind as a prime example. Why are we spending billions to bid up the prices of farm commodities above what the domestic or world market is willing to pay? The result is a waste of food that would be recognized immediately as criminal if it arose in any other context. Only a government program could succeed in transforming the breadbasket of the world into a net importer of food. Nevertheless, the realities of special interest politics are such that spending cutbacks of the magnitude that would be required to eliminate the deficit are remote indeed, Gramm-Rudman-Hollings or no. At best we will see a gradual shrinkage of the deficit as the growth of the economy during the next decade outpaces the growth of government programs, allowing tax revenues to catch up again with expenditures.

The Bottom Line

A widening gap between federal government spending and tax revenues has produced record-breaking deficits since 1982. The immediate cause is the Economic Recovery Tax Act of 1981 which cut taxes for both individuals and businesses. Supply-siders argued that the additional incentives for work and investment provided by lower tax rates would raise the level of economic activity enough to make up the loss of tax revenue. The government would be ahead by collecting a smaller fraction of a larger pie. So far, it hasn't worked out that way. The long run problem in controlling the deficit is that government spending has tended to rise as a fraction of GNP while tax revenue has not. The federal government now spends about 25 percent of the GNP, due mainly to the growth of transfer payments since the mid-1960s. The most realistic hope for controlling the deficit is probably that the growth in spending may be held down sufficiently for the rest of the economy to catch up over the next decade.

12

The Other Deficit:
Our Foreign Trade Gap

International trade has never been as important to the U.S. economy as it has been to Europe and Japan because America contains within its borders almost all the elements of a complete economic system—mining and petroleum, basic metallurgical industry, manufacturing, agriculture, financial services, and transportation to connect them. The domestic economy is so huge that all of these industries can grow very large and efficient without requiring foreign markets. Europe needed to create the Common Market to achieve the kind of scale and diversity within one economy that the U.S. has by itself. There is no doubt in my mind that this is one of the most important reasons for the spectacular success of the U.S. economy over the past century. It also accounts for the fact that international trade has never received the kind of attention from American economists that it always has in Canada or Europe. Until recently, it has been possible to talk about economic affairs as if the U.S. economy were the only economy in the world, and usually get by with it. No longer.

Since World War II, the U.S. economy has been gradually becoming more integrated with the world economy, but this development has become inescapably evident only in the last decade. The Arab oil embargo of late 1973 and the ensuing energy crisis were the first signals to most Americans that our days of economic isolation were over. The fact that a small group of oil producers half a world away (depicted in cartoons as a bunch of sheiks sitting on camels) could bring the L.A. freeways to a halt was profoundly disconcerting. Many simply refused to believe it. The energy crisis was artificial, engineered by American oil companies to jack up prices—so went this ostrich school of thought. (Funny that oil stocks took a beating.) It was more comforting to believe that our big companies were still in control of the oil market, that foreigners simply didn't have the economic clout to pull off something like this. It is interesting that this theory never took hold in Europe or Japan, and I think that is because people in those countries were long aware of their growing dependence on Middle East oil. They never had been under the illusion that they were self-sufficient.

A more subtle process that is inexorably transforming our role in the world economy is the industrialization of the rest of the world. We simply are no longer the best at doing almost everything as we were in the years following World War II. We emerged from the war with our industries intact and with a long lead in most areas of technology. Gradually, our technology has spread through the industrialized world, thanks in great part to direct foreign investment by our own companies. Indeed in some fields the lead has shifted abroad. International specialization now makes more sense as a way of exploiting the "comparative advantage" of each trading nation. The United States has a comparative advantage in sophisticated products such as large computers and aircraft that make use of cutting-edge technology. This is the type of product we will export. Asian countries have a comparative advantage in manufacturing consumer electronics that depends on established technology but requires substantial labor in assembly. They will sell us microwave ovens and stereo equipment, and we will sell them 747's. This process of trade on the basis of comparative advantage benefits us all and has contributed greatly to the incredible rise in living standards that has occurred virtually worldwide during the past 40 years. That the U.S. has become part of this world economy is natural and inevitable, and we reap enormous benefits from our participation in it.

Throughout the 1960s and early 1970s world trade grew rapidly, and we both imported and exported increasing quantities of goods. The difference between the dollar value of goods exported and the value of goods imported is called the Merchandise Trade Balance. When we earn more by exporting than we spend on imports, we have a trade surplus. This is what we had until the mid-1970s. What did we do with this surplus? We invested it abroad. There is no point in just putting all those Deutsche marks, francs, and pounds under our mattresses; instead we invested them. We built plants abroad, lent to foreign governments and firms through our banks, and purchased foreign securities. This was precisely the process that allowed the world economy to rebuild after the war.

Then in the late 1970s, we started to run a deficit in our trade activities. We were spending more on imports than we were earning from exports. This was largely due to the enormous rise in payments to the OPEC countries to pay for our oil imports starting

171

in 1974. OPEC in turn "recycled" their extra dollars by purchasing investment assets in the U.S.. Selling Treasury bills, real estate, and stocks to dollar-laden sheiks became big business. The OPEC countries soon learned how to spend most of their dollar surplus, and by the end of the 1970s it looked like our trade deficit might be on the way to disappearing again. Then in 1982 something drastic happened. The Merchandise Trade Balance lost its balance, and we were suddenly running a staggering trade deficit.

The suddenness of this change is seen in Figure 47 where the Merchandise Trade Balance is plotted for the past quarter century. Look familiar? It bears a close resemblance to the picture of the federal budget deficit that we saw in Figure 41. Both deficits fell off a cliff at about the same time. Is this a coincidence? Not likely, but more about that later. The Merchandise Trade Balance is a monthly indicator, and is reported near the end of the following month. It is expressed in millions of dollars for that month; it is not expressed as an annual rate like many other indicators. As you can see, during 1985 it was running at about $11,000 million per month which is about $132 billion at an annual rate. That is not quite as big as the Federal Budget Deficit which was over $200 billion for 1985, but it is right up there as scary numbers go. If we looked at imports and exports separately we would see that imports continued to grow in the 1980s, but exports suddenly stopped growing. Have we lost our competitive edge? Are we the victims of predatory price-cutting by foreign competitors? Are foreign governments unfairly depriving our products of access to their markets? These are the questions most often put forward in the press, and to some extent the answers are "yes" to each. But none of these factors underwent an abrupt

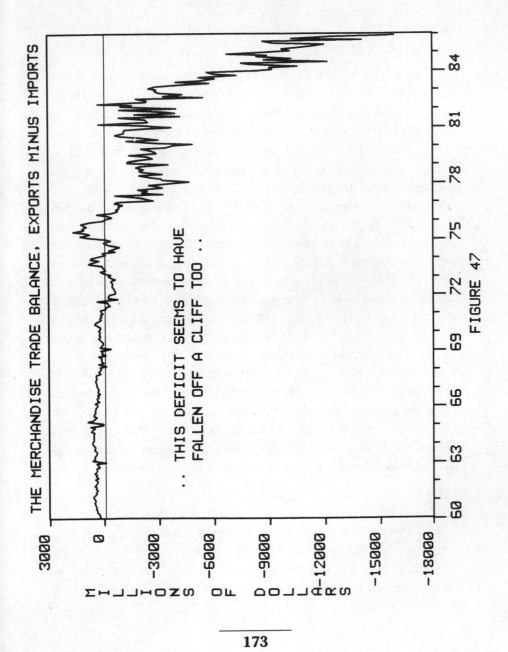

THE MERCHANDISE TRADE BALANCE, EXPORTS MINUS IMPORTS

.. THIS DEFICIT SEEMS TO HAVE
FALLEN OFF A CLIFF TOO ..

FIGURE 47

MILLIONS OF DOLLARS

3000
0
-3000
-6000
-9000
-12000
-15000
-18000

60   63   66   69   72   75   78   81   84

change in 1982 that would explain why the trade balance suddenly fell out of bed.

One factor that did change abruptly in 1982 was the value of the U.S. dollar on foreign exchange markets. Most of us think about exchange rates only when we travel abroad. Getting ready for that trip to France in 1984, you stopped at the foreign exchange counter at your bank to inquire about buying some French francs. You were told that your U.S. dollar would buy 10 of them. This was good news because when you went to France a few years ago you only got 5 francs for each dollar. The dollar had doubled in value in terms of francs in only five years, a big change. Although France had had a bit more inflation than the U.S. since your last trip, you were able to buy a lot more in France this time, or spend considerably less. In fact, this is one of the main reasons why you decided to travel to France instead of going to San Francisco. A lot of people were making just this sort of calculation, not only in francs but in Deutsche marks, pounds, and yen. They were comparing not only the cost of travel but of imported cars, clothing, machine tools, and strawberry jam. If the dollar is high-priced relative to other currencies, we find it attractive to buy their goods, but they find ours costly. In 1984, a lot of foreigners were deciding not to buy our machinery, grain, and electronics because the cost to them of anything made in the U.S.A. had about doubled in the span of a few years.

Of course, the dollar will not rise or fall against all currencies at the same time or by the same amount. To get a picture of the overall value of the dollar against the currencies that matter in trade, we can use an average where each currency is weighted by the volume of trade it represents. This indicator is charted in Figure 48 and it clearly shows a dramatic reversal in the fortunes

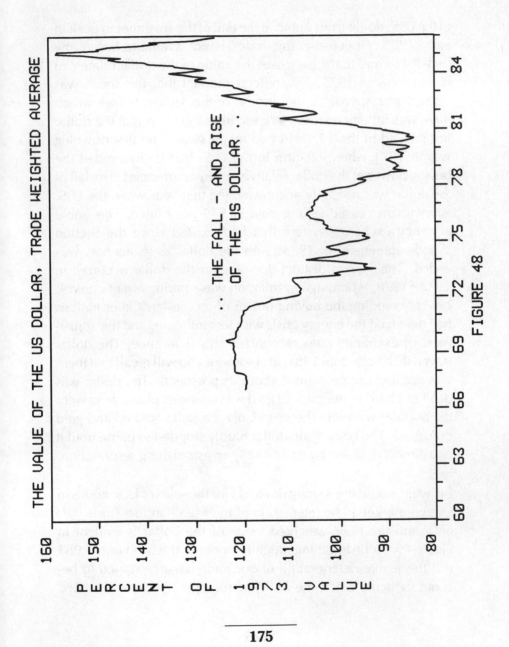

THE VALUE OF THE US DOLLAR, TRADE WEIGHTED AVERAGE

.. THE FALL – AND RISE OF THE US DOLLAR ..

FIGURE 48

of the U.S. dollar from slump at the end of the seventies to peak in early 1985. Notice that this index is not available before the mid-1960s and that it expresses the value of the dollar relative to what it was in 1973. This reflects the fact that this index was created in response to the turmoil of the 1970s, before which there was little need for it. We see from the chart that the dollar lost ground in the 1970s in two major steps. The first downleg was in 1971 when inflation in the U.S. had badly eroded the buying power of the dollar relative to other currencies. The fall of the dollar was officially acknowledged that year when the U.S. government ceased selling gold at $35 per ounce. The stable currency exchange system that had existed since the Bretton Woods agreement of 1944, with the dollar as its anchor, was ended. The second distinct downleg for the dollar occurred in 1977–1978, when, again, inflation was running out of control, severely eroding the buying power of the dollar. Other nations had managed the energy crisis with less inflation, and the adjustment of exchange rates recognized this difference. The dollar stayed in the pits until 1981, and some of you will recall that there was nothing but pessimism about its prospects. The dollar was dead as a hard currency, and gold was taking its place, or so went the popular wisdom. Then suddenly the dollar soared and gold collapsed. The born-again dollar hardly stopped to pause until it had almost doubled by early 1985, an astonishing resurrection.

But what would the soaring dollar do for the sales of U.S. goods in foreign markets? The interaction of the Merchandise Trade Balance and the trade-weighted value of the dollar is evident in Figure 49. At first nothing much happened. It wasn't until 1983 that the severe deterioration of our trade balance started to become evident. Once the ball got rolling, it picked up speed

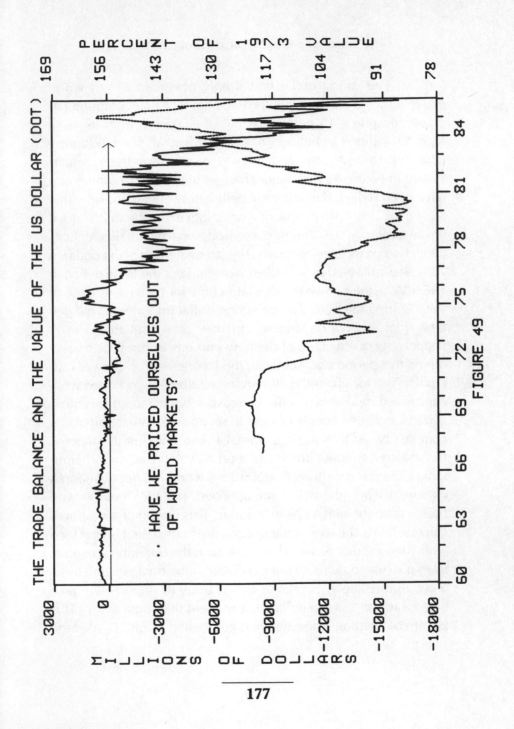

THE TRADE BALANCE AND THE VALUE OF THE US DOLLAR (DOT)

... HAVE WE PRICED OURSELVES OUT OF WORLD MARKETS?

FIGURE 49

rapidly. The strong dollar had simply priced us out of world markets. At the end of 1985, the trade balance was continuing its plunge despite a 15 percent retreat of the dollar from its 1984 high. Why didn't a cheaper dollar in 1985 make our goods more attractive to foreigners and help to narrow our trade deficit? Notice in Figure 49 that major changes in the value of the dollar have been reflected in the trade deficit only after a considerable lag, on the order of a couple of years. Notice that the sharp retreat of the dollar in 1977–1978 was followed by smaller deficits about two years later. Similarly, the strengthening of the dollar in 1981 was followed by a marked worsening of the trade deficit in 1983. Why the two-year lag? It takes time for patterns of trade to shift. During the period of the strong dollar importers expanded their dealer networks and set up new ones, but this doesn't happen overnight. One of the new entrants in the U.S. market during this period was Komatsu, the Japanese equivalent of Caterpillar Tractor. To sell earthmoving equipment you need well-capitalized dealers who offer effective service and an inventory of parts. It takes a couple of years to set up an organization of that complexity. At this writing, Komatsu is rethinking its strategy, faced with a stronger dollar and a rejuvenated Caterpillar. Similarly, Caterpillar customers around the world did not abandon it overnight when the dollar strengthened, nor will they be won back overnight with a cheaper dollar. This period of adjustment can result in a cheaper dollar making the trade deficit bigger for a while instead of smaller. This is because the quantity of exports takes a while to increase but the dollar value on a per-unit basis drops immediately. Similarly, the quantity of imports will take time to adjust, but the dollar cost of them rises right away. This pattern of "getting worse before it gets better" is often called the

J-curve. Next time you hear that term from some economist being interviewed on the evening business news, you will know what it means and why.

We have seen that the soaring dollar seems to have a lot to do with the trade deficit of the mid-1980s, but what has been pushing up the value of the dollar on foreign exchange markets? When the price of anything goes up it is because more of it is demanded or less of it is being supplied. Both explanations apply in the case of the dollar. We saw in Chapter 3 that a more restrictive monetary policy designed to kill inflation was taking hold in the U.S. in the early 1980s. The Federal Reserve was reducing the supply of dollars, at least relative to the growth of the economy. Secondly, foreigners were finding investment in the U.S. unusually attractive and were demanding dollars to buy U.S. securities. Recall that we showed in Chapter 4 that real interest rates, the return on a bill or bond net of inflation, shot up to unprecedented levels in 1981. Suddenly, investment in very safe U.S. Treasury bills and bonds offered an extraordinarily high rate of return, specially to untaxed foreign investors. We see the interaction of real interest rates, represented by the real rate of return on U.S. Treasury bills, and the trade-weighted value of the dollar in Figure 50. The real interest rate, the dotted line, drops below zero in 1973 and pretty much stays there for the duration of that decade. That was also a period of weakness for the dollar. Then in 1980, the real return on Treasury bills jumps very suddenly to the high plateau that it holds for the next five years. The dollar follows along, peaking in early 1985 as real interest rates in the U.S. started to ease.

When we first looked at the Merchandise Trade Balance in Figure 47 we noticed that it looks very much like the federal budget

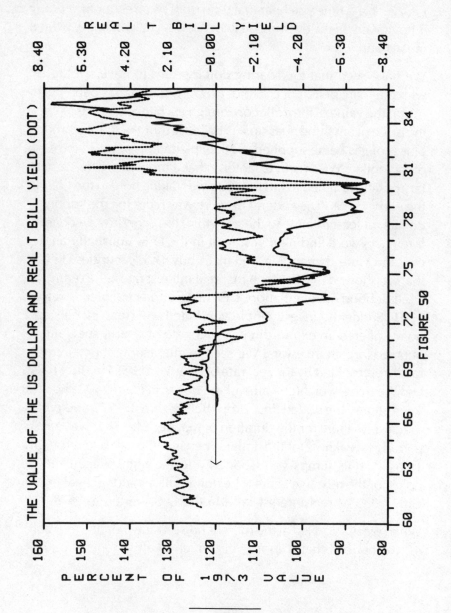

THE VALUE OF THE US DOLLAR AND REAL T BILL YIELD (DOT)

FIGURE 50

deficit, and we guessed that that is not a coincidence. Therein lies the final piece of this puzzle. Why were real interest rates so high in the 1980s and why did they persist so long? The Fed's anti-inflation policy got the ball rolling in 1980, but there can be little doubt that the bulging deficit in the federal budget following the 1981 tax cuts are what kept it rolling. The U.S. Treasury started dumping about $200 billion per year of new bills and bonds on the market. How could this massive supply of securities be absorbed? Interest rates had to rise in real terms to induce investors to hold more Treasury securities than they otherwise would have. These high real rates of return attracted foreign investors, too. They wanted to participate in this high-yield bonanza by increasing their holdings of U.S. securities. As they stepped up their purchase of U.S. dollars to pay for American securities, they bid up the value of the dollar relative to pounds, Deutsche marks, yen, and Swiss francs. The soaring dollar priced U.S. goods out of foreign markets, producing the trade deficit. It was this trade deficit that gave foreigners the means to increase their holdings of U.S. securities because they were earning $132 billion more per year from exports to the U.S. than they were spending on imports. This is how the trade deficit was financing about two-thirds of the federal budget deficit. In effect, we were trading U.S. Treasury bills, stocks, and bonds for BMW's and fine French wines. This way the yuppies got their BMW's and their French wines and the supply-siders got their tax cuts.

Can we expect that the cheaper dollar that emerged at the end of 1985 would eliminate the trade deficit? Not likely as long as the federal government continues to run a big deficit. That continuing flow of additional Treasury securities coming to market to finance the budget deficit will tend to keep real interest rates in the U.S. relatively high, so that foreigners are going to continue to want to trade their goods for our debt. This means that we will continue to buy more from abroad than we sell abroad. The size of the trade deficit will depend, too, on how interest rates move in other major industrial countries and on the policies of our Federal Reserve that influence our interest rates. But there is little chance that we will finance our huge budget deficit entirely without foreign help.

But what about all those television programs about the trade deficit that take you to Japan and show you how their government puts all sorts of barriers in the way of our goods? Certainly the Japanese do protect their home industries from foreign competition, and this reduces sales of American products there. Cherries can't be imported until the Japanese crop has been sold. Cars imported to Japan have to undergo rigorous inspection that is not required of Japanese cars arriving here. There are a lot of examples like these, and they suggest that we could sell a lot more goods there if we were allowed to compete on an equal footing. This would be better for everybody, most of all the long-suffering Japanese consumer (imagine having to pay five dollars a pound for cherries at the height of the season!). But it probably would have little if any effect on our trade deficit with Japan. Our increased earning of yen from our exports would be spent on more imports from Japan, and the Japanese would continue to use their trade surplus to buy American securities for their portfolios. We should all be in favor of free trade because it makes the world economy more efficient, not because it would eliminate our trade deficit.

The Other Deficit: Our Foreign Trade Gap

The Bottom Line

Foreigners have helped to finance our federal budget deficit by stepping up their purchase of American securities. They have done this not because they like us, but because our interest rates have been so high. They get the dollars to buy our debt by selling more goods to us than they purchase from us. This gives us a trade deficit but gives foreigners the means to lend us about two-thirds of what we need to cover the federal deficit.

The Calendar of Important Indicators[a]
A Typical Month

1	2 Manufacturers' Orders	3	4 Auto sales	5 Unemployment Rate
8 Purchasing Management Survey	9	10	11 M1 and M2	12 Producer Price Index Retail Sales
15 Industrial Production	16 Capacity Utilization	17 Housing Starts	18	19 GNP Corporate Profits
22 Personal Income	23 Consumer Price Index	24	25	26
29	30 Index of Leading Indicators Merchandise Trade Balance			

[a]All of these indicators refer to results for the prior month except GNP and Corporate Profits which are quarterly. Preliminary estimates for GNP are released the month following the end of the calendar quarter and revised figures are released each of the next two months on roughly the same date. Corporate Profits are released in the second month following the end of the calendar quarter and a revised estimate is released in the third month.

Index

Accountants' profits, 90
Aid to Families with Dependent Children, 145
Assets, inflation-sensitive *vs.* financial, 42
Availability, as criterion for choosing economic indicators, 4

Bank accounts, interest-bearing, 100
Banks, deregulation, 37–38
Bonds
investing in, 19
see also Treasury bonds
Budget deficit, *see* Deficit, budget

Capital consumption adjustment, 76
CCA, 76
Certificate of deposit, 8
Charts:
Figure 1: 90-day treasury bills as indicators of short term interest rates, 12
Figure 2: Treasury bonds as indicators of long term interest rates, 14
Figure 3: Comparison of long term and short term interest rates, 16
Figure 4: Predicting direction of interest rates, 18
Figure 5: Change in consumer prices as indicator of inflation, 23
Figure 6: Changes in producer prices as indicator of inflation, 25
Figure 7: Inflation as measured by Dow Jones Commodity Spot Price Index, 27
Figure 8: Rate of change in money supply, 33
Figure 9: Relationship of money supply growth and inflation, 35
Figure 10: Comparison of T-bill yield and inflation rate, 41
Figure 11: Treasury bill yield less inflation indicates real interest rate, 43

185

Index

Charts (*Continued*)

Figure 12: Immediate *vs.* long-term effect of money growth on interest rates, 46

Figure 13: Standard and Poor's 500 Index and growth of market portfolio, 50

Figure 14: Indicator of real stock market value, 52

Figure 15: Response of stocks to inflation, 1961-1985, 54

Figure 16: Gross National Product as indicator of real economy, 61

Figure 17: Index of Industrial Production as indicator of real economy, 63

Figure 18: Capacity utilization in manufacturing as indicator of real economy, 66

Figure 19: Profits of U.S. corporations before and after taxes, 72

Figure 20: Corporate profits after taxes in constant dollars, 74

Figure 21: Corporate profits after taxes with IVA and CCA in 1982 dollars, 78

Figure 22: Really real profits *vs.* capacity utilization, 80

Figure 23: Interaction of stock market and real profits over last 25 years, 86

Figure 24: P/R ratio of Standard & Poor's 500 stock index, 91

Figure 25: Index of Leading Indicators and Index of Industrial Production, 98

Figure 26: Real quantity of M2 and industrial production, 102

Figure 27: Growth rates of real money and of industrial production, 104

Figure 28: Standard & Poor's Stock Index and industrial production, 107

Figure 29: Real Standard & Poor's 500 Stock Index and industrial production, 110

Figure 30: Housing starts and Index of Industrial Production, 113

Figure 31: Initial unemployment claims and industrial production, 115

Figure 32: Manufacturers' orders and industrial production, 117

Figure 33: Consumer Price Index inflation rates lead real Standard & Poor's 500, 122

Figure 34: Change in inflation leads real Standard & Poor's 500, 124

Figure 35: Yield on Treasury bills leads Standard & Poor's 500, 126

Figure 36: Change in Treasury bill yield leads Standard & Poor's 500, 128

Figure 37: Spread between long and short term interest rates as useful indicator for stock market timing, 130

Figure 38: Spread between long and short term interest rates as compared with Standard & Poor's 500, 132

Figure 39: Change in Producer Price Index leads real Standard & Poor's 500, 135

Figure 40: Change in growth rate of real M2 leads real Standard & Poor's 500, 139

Figure 41: Budget deficit of U.S. government, 144

Figure 42: Federal budget deficit adjusted for inflation, 146

Figure 43: Federal budget deficit as percent of Gross National Product, 148

Figure 44: Federal deficit as percentage of Gross National Product compared to Rate of Capacity Utilization, 150

Index

Figure 45: Federal spending and federal
revenues as a percentage of Gross
National Product, 162
Figure 46: Three categories of federal
spending as percentages of Gross
National Product, 165
Figure 47: Merchandise trade balance,
1960-1985, 173
Figure 48: Value of U.S. dollar using
trade-weighted average, 175
Figure 49: Trade balance and value of
the U.S. dollar, 177
Figure 50: Interaction of real interest
rates and trade-weighted value of
dollar, 180
use of, in interpreting economic
indicators, 2, 4
Checking accounts
market interest accounts, 37
Commodities.
monitoring prices, 26–27
prices, as indicator of inflation,
26–28, 53
and stock market timing, 125, 134
see also Dow Jones Commodity Spot
Price Index
Common stock, 70
Comparative advantage, trade on basis
of, 170–171
Competition, foreign industrial, 88–89
Constant dollars, 71
Consmer Price Index, 21–23, 85
Corporate Profits After Taxes with IVA and
CCA and CCA in Constant Dollars,
76
Cost of living, and relationship to real
value of stock portfolios, 51–53
CPI, see Consumer Price Index
Crowding out, 157

Deficit
budget, 5, 88
and adjusting for inflation, 145
causes, 143–161
crowding-out effect, 157
and Economic Recovery Tax Act of
1981, 149, 151
effects, 156–157
on inflation, 159–161
financing, 159–161
and growth in transfer payments,
164–167
measurement, as percent of Gross
National Product, 147, 148
prospects for eliminating, 161–167
rate, 147
and Ricardo's theory, 158–159
and special interest politics, 167
and supply-side theory of federal
finance, 151–156
and upward trend in spending, 161,
163–164
federal, see Deficit, budget
foreign trade, 5
and importance of foreign trade to
U.S. economy, 169–171
and international specialization,
170–171
relationship, to federal budget
deficit, 181–183
Deflation, 4, 24
Depreciation:
and historical cost vs. replacement
cost, 75–76
and how inflation distorts profits, 79
understatement, and overstated
earnings, 92
Deregulation:
in areas of U.S. economy, 89
of banking industry, 111
Disinflation, 45, 79
Dividends, 69–70, 83
Dow Jones Commodity Futures Price
Index, 26, 134–135
Dow Jones Commodity Spot Price Index,
26, 134–135
as leading indicator of inflation,
26–28

Index

Dow Jones Industrial Average, as
    indicator of stock market value,
    49, 106

Earnings, 70. *See also* Profits
Earnings yield, 92
"Easy money" policies, 5
Economic indicators, *see* Indicators,
    economic
Economic Recovery Tax Act of 1981,
    79, 163, 167
Economics, academic, 2
Economists, mainstream *vs.* supply-
    siders, 151–156
Economy, interaction of monetary
    economy with real economy, 5,
    140
Economy, real, *see* Real economy
Energy crisis, 85, 89, 170
    effect of:
        on economy, 34
        on inflation, 42
ERTA, *see* Economic Recovery Tax Act
    of 1981
Exchange rate, and foreign trade deficit,
    174–179
Expectations:
    of future stock market growth, 93
    regarding U.S. economy, 87–88
    role, in investing, 15, 17, 19

Farm program, 166–167
Fed, *see* Federal Reserve Board
Federal debt, 143–144. *See also* Deficit,
    budget
Federal government, expanded regulatory
    role, 106
Federal Reserve Bank:
    actions to control inflation, 89
        and relationship to stock prices, 123
    and actions to curb inflation in late
        1979, 136
    and increasing liquidity of banking
        system to lower interest rates, 111

and lowering interest rates to stimulate
    economy, 125
policies, and role of politics and
    elections, 140–141
"printing press," 159, 160
raising interest rates to reduce inflation,
    125
and reducing liquidity of banking
    system to raise interest rates, 109,
    111
see also Federal Reserve Board
Federal Reserve Board, 38
    and actions to increase money supply,
        31–34, 42
    and actions to reduce money supply,
        37–38
    and "easy money" policies, 5
    and liquidity, 101, 103
    and money supply numbers, 4
    and "tight money" policies, 24
    see also Federal Reserve Bank
Fixed income securities, 7
Foreign trade deficit, *see* Deficit, foreign
    trade
Freidman, Milton, 34, 105, 155
"Friedman surge," 34–35
Futures prices, 26. *See also* Dow Jones
    Commodity Futures Price Index

GNP, *see* Gross National Product
Goods and services, 164–167
Gramm-Rudman-Hollings law, 161, 167
Great Depression, 64, 105, 136
GRH, *see* Gramm-Rudman-Hollings law
Gross National Product, 67
    conceptual and practical problems in
        measuring, 58–60
    defined, 58
    as measure of inflation, 60
    real *vs.* nominal, 60
    timeliness of, 59–60

Health insurance, 166–167
    and Federal budget deficit, 164

188

Index

Housing industry:
  housing permits, 112
  housing starts, 112, 118
  indicators of housing activity, 112
  as leading indicator of economy, 111
  sensitivity, to interest rates, 111

Identification problem, 158
Income tax, and supply-side theory,
  151–156
Indexation, 149
Index of Industrial Production, 65, 67
  as indicator of real economy, 62–64
Index of Leading Indicators:
  accuracy, as forecaster of real
    economy, 97
  components, 95–97, 106
  defined, 95
  meaning of growth rate, 95–96
  shortcomings, 97–99
  value, in forecasting direction of
    economy, 118
Indicators, economic, 1–5
  calendar of important indicators, 184
  criteria for choosing, 3–4
  importance of interpreting in context
    of surrounding events, 136–137,
    141
  Index of Leading Indicators vs.
    individual leading indicators, 118
  indicators for stock market timing, 5
  indicators to watch, 5
  leading indicators:
    defined, 5
    most timely, 100
  overrated indicators, 112–117
Inflation, 4
  adjustment for, when measuring real
    value of stock market, 85
  control, through reducing growth rate
    of money supply, 36–38
  defined, 21
  and distortion of corporate profits,
    73–75, 76, 79, 81

double-digit, and response of Federal
    Reserve Bank, 89
and Economic Recovery Tax Act of
    1981, 163–164
and effect of growth in money supply,
    44–45
and fall in value of U.S. dollar, 176
as indicator of future direction of stock
    market, 55
inflation premium, 44
and inverse relationship between infla-
    tion and stock prices, 120–123
and investing in money market funds,
    55
measuring, 21–22
and money supply, 30
Producer Price Index as leading
    indicator of inflation, 134–137
rate, 21
relationship, to liquidity, 101, 103
and role of depreciation in distorting
    corporate profits, 76
using changes, for timing stock
    purchases, 123–125
Inflation premium, 44
Initial Unemployment Claims, value, as
    leading economic indicator, 112,
    114
Interest rates:
  and balancing long term against
    anticipated short term rates, 17
  causes of high interest rates, 157–158
  defined, 7
  history, 11
  and housing industry, 111
  and immediate vs. long-term effect of
    growth in money supply, 45–46
  predicting future direction, 17–19
  real interest rates, 4–5, 40–42, 47
    and foreign investment in U.S., 181
  real vs. nominal, 39, 40, 44
  relationship, to inflation, 39
  and Ricardo's theory, 158–159
  role, in investing, 7–19

189

Index

Interest rates (*Continued*)
  and spread between short and long
    term rates, 17–19
  as stock market timing indicator,
    129–133
  as stock market timing indicator,
    125–129
  T-bill yield as indicator of real interest
    rate, 42–43
Inventories, and distortion of inflation on
    profits, 79
Inventory valuation adjustment, 75
Investing:
  in bonds, 19
  foreign investment in U.S., 179
  and role of expectations in, 15, 17, 19
  rules, 123, 125, 136–137
  and use of experts, 2–3
Investors, beliefs, as reflected in stock
    market, 108
IVA, 75

Jargon, economic 2, 3
J curve, 178–179

Keynesians, theory of causes of recessions
    and depressions, 105
Kuznets, Simon, 58

Laffer, Arthur, 154–156
Laffer curve, 154, 155
Leading economic indicators, *see* Index
    of Leading Indicators; Indicators,
    economic
Liquidity:
  defined, 100
  and growth rate of economy,
    103–105
  and inflation, 101, 103
  as leading indicator of economic
    activity, 100–101
  measurement, 100
  swings in, 101–103

using changes in growth rate, as
    indicator for stock market timing,
    138–140
Loans, mortgage, 111
Long term yield, 7

M1, 32, 100
M2:
  defined, 32, 37–38
  as leading economic indicator,
    100–101
  real M2, 100–101, 105
  using real M2 as leading indicator of
    stock market direction, 138–140
  value, as leading indicator of
    economy, 118
Manufacturers' new orders for consumer
    goods, value, as leading indicator,
    116–117
Martin, William McChesney, 109
Media:
  and announcement of Rate of Capacity
    Utilization, 65
  and coverage of supply-side theory of
    federal finance, 154–156
  financial coverage in, 58
  and reporting:
    Dow Jones Spot and Futures Indices,
      136
  and reporting economic indicators,
    2–3
  and reporting foreign trade deficit, 172
  and reporting Index of Leading
    Indicators, 95, 99
  and reporting unemployment claims,
    114
Medicaid, 164, 166
Medicare, 164, 166
Merchandise Trade Balance, 171, 172,
    179, 181
Monetarism, 34–35
Monetarists, theory of causes of
    recessions and depressions, 105
Monetary economics, paradox, 44–45

Index

Monetary economy, 5
Money, 29–30
    circulation, in banking system, 31–32
    defined, 38
    power, to move economy, 104, 105
    see also Money supply
Money market, 30
Money market mutual funds, 13, 100
Money market security, 7
Money supply:
    defined, 29–30, 32, 38
    effect:
        of growth in, on inflation, 44–45
        of sharp acceleration in, 45
        of sharp slowdown in, 45
    growth in, as leading indicator of
        inflation, 34
    growth of, 32–34
    and inflation, 30–31
    as measured by M2, 97
    reducing rate of growth in, 36–37
    reliability, as economic indicator, 38
Money supply numbers, 4
Mortgage loans, 11

National Bureau of Economic Research,
    105
National debt, 143–144, 166. See also
    Deficit, budget
National defense, 164–167

Oil crisis, effect, on inflation, 40
Oil embargo, 34, 64, 85, 170
Oil prices, 34, 64, 89, 123
OPEC, 34, 53, 64, 79, 85, 103, 171–
    172

P/E ratio:
    defined, 90
    and expectation of increase in, 93
    as real indicator of stock market,
        90–93
PPI, see Producer Price Index
Preferred stock, 69–70

Press, financial, see Media
Price to earnings ratio, see P/E ratio
Producer Price Index:
    defined, 24, 134
    as indicator for stock market timing,
        134–137
    as leading indicator of inflation,
        24–26
Production, industrial production relative
        to production capacity, and perfor-
        mance of real economy, 65
Profits:
    accountants' profits, 90
    adjustment to, via capital consumption
        adjustment, 76
    before vs. after taxes, 71–73
    defined, 69
    expected growth in corporate profits,
        93
    and growth rate from mid-1960's to
        1984, 88
    how inflation creates illusory profits,
        example, 73–75
    illusory inflation profits and taxes, 73,
        75
    impact of real profits on stock market,
        83–93
    inflation-caused illusory profits and
        overstated earnings, 92
    measurement, distorted by inflation,
        73, 75, 76, 79, 81
    and real increase in purchasing
        power, 71
    relationship, to real economy, 70, 79,
        79, 81, 81
    and removing distortion of inflation,
        73
    role of accounting methods in creating
        illusory profits, 74–75, 81
    sensitivity, to real economy, 79, 81

Random walk theory, 120
Rate of Capacity Utilization, 65, 79
Rate of inflation, 21

191

Index

Real economy, 57–67
  and capacity utilization in
    manufacturing as indicator, 65–66
  and corporate profits, 79, 81
  defined, 5, 57, 67
  indicators that forecast, 95–118
  measurement:
    via Gross National Product, 67
    via Index of Industrial Production,
      67
  relationship, to profits, 70, 79–80
Real income, 57
Real M2, see M2
Recession, 103, 105
  1967 recession, 145
  1970–1971 recession, 145
  in 1970s, 67
  of 1973-1975, 85, 87, 103, 145
  of 1980, 87, 145
  of 1981-1982, 87, 108, 109, 136,
    145, 153
  defined, 61–62
  historical picture, 62–64
  and housing starts, 112
  recession-level deficits, 147, 149
  relationship, to federal budget deficit,
    145, 147
Release, timely, as criterion for choosing
  economic indicators, 3–4
Relevance, as criterion for choosing
  economic indicators, 3
Ricardo, David, 158–159, 160
Ricardo's theory, 158–159

Samuelson, Paul, 108
Schwartz, Anna, 105
Securities:
  difference between short term and
    long term, 10–11
  fixed income, 7
  short term, 7
Short term yield, 7
Social security, 164, 166
Spot prices, 26. See also Dow Jones

Commodity Spot Price Index
Spread:
  negative, 129
  positive, 129
Stability, as criterion for choosing
  economic indicators, 4
Standard & Poor's 500 Stock Index, 85
  as indicator of stock market value,
    49–50
  as leading indicator of economy, 106
  1973–1982 losses, 53
  P/E ratio, 90–91
  real index as leading indicator of real
    economy, 108–109
Stock dividends, 69–70, 83
Stock market:
  assessing real performance, 51–53
  collapse, in 1970s, 84–85, 93
  and corporate profits, 69
  difficulty of forecasting, 119–120
  improving timing indicators for,
    133–141
  and indicator of real value of stock
    portfolio, 51–53
  and indicators for stock market timing,
    119–141
  interaction, with real profits, 85–94
  and inverse relationship between
    inflation and stock prices,
    120–123
  investments in, 5
  as leading indicator of economy, 106
  and loss of confidence in U.S.
    economy, 90, 92
  major shifts in, 106, 108
  as predictor of moves in real economy,
    106, 108
  promise of future growth, 89–90, 93
  random walk theory, 120
  rebirth, in 1985, 70
  relationship:
    to real economic growth, 64, 65
    to real economy, 57–58
  reliability, as leading indicator of
    economy, 106

Index

responsiveness, to profits, 87
rules of investing in, 123, 125,
    136–137
seasonal patterns in, 120
and social attitudes toward American
    business, 84–85, 88
stagnation period of late 1960s to early
    1980s, 70, 77
using changes in inflation for timing
    stock purchases, 123–125
using interest rate spread for timing
    stock market purchases, 129–133
using M2 as stock market timing
    indicator, 138–140
value, as leading indicator of
    economy, 118
Stocks:
    defined, 69
    kinds, 69–70
    poor performance of industrial stocks,
        65
    potential, for real appreciation in
        value, 53
    as protection against inflation, 49, 51,
        53–55
    relationship, to real economy, 67
    reliability of real value, 109
    stock prices as leading indicator, 97
    see also Stock market
Supply-side theory, 151–156, 167

Taxation, and supply-side theory,
    151–156
Tax bracket, 163
Taxes:
    corporate, corporate profits after taxes,
        70–77

government tax revenue compared to
    government spending, 143–145
illusory profits and income tax, 75–76
"Tight money" policies, 24
Timeliness, 3–4
Timing, indicators for stock market
    timing, 119–141
Trade balance, J curve, 178–179
Transfer payments, 164
Treasury bills, 8–9, 111
    change in yield, as stock market timing
        indicator, 125–129
    creditworthiness, 8–9
    defined, 8
    and relationship to short term interest
        rates, 8–9
Treasury bonds, 9–10
    relationship of bond prices to yields,
        9–10
    and relationship to long term interest
        rates, 9–10

Unemployment insurance, 145

Value added, 58
Volcker, Paul, 37–38, 136

Welfare payments, 164
Welfare programs, 145, 166
Wholesale Price Index, see Producer
    Price Index

Yield, 7